SHAKESPEARE'S STRANGEST TALES

Other titles in the STRANGEST series

SHAKESPEARE'S STRANGEST® TALES

Extraordinary but true tales from 400 years
of Shakespearean theatre

IAIN SPRAGG

PORTICO

First published in the United Kingdom in 2016 by
Portico
1 Gower Street
London
WC1E 6HD

An imprint of Pavilion Books Company Ltd

ISBN 978-1-91023-290-3

A CIP catalogue record for this book is available from the British Library.

10 9 8 7 6 5 4 3 2 1

Reproduction by ColourDepth UK
Printed and bound by Bookwell, Finland

Illustrations by Matthew Booker

This book can be ordered direct from the publisher at www.pavilionbooks.com

CONTENTS

'Tis wondrous strange, the like yet never heard of.

(Henry VI Part III, *Act II, Scene I*)

INTRODUCTION

The greatest writer in the English language the world has ever seen, William Shakespeare remains a cultural phenomenon 400 years after his death and his plays and sonnets are some of the most celebrated and widely read works in the world of literature.

The Bard's humble beginnings in Stratford-upon-Avon belie the incredible global popularity his dramatic work has gone on to achieve over the last four centuries, and although he is one of England's favourite sons, he is also arguably its greatest ever export. His plays have been performed in every country in the world, his cumulative audience now number in the billions, and some of his iconic lines are the most quoted dramatic words in human history.

For such a famous figure however, we know surprisingly little about his life, but what we do know makes for fascinating reading, and in *Shakespeare's Strangest Tales* we delve deep into the more surprising chapters of the Bard's work, his life story and the weird and wonderful tales his dramas have inspired. And so, in the pages that follow, we will unearth the real reason the character of Falstaff failed to make an appearance in *Henry V*, which play our Will hastily scribbled to avoid becoming embroiled in the fallout of the Gunpowder Plot and why the first recorded performance of *Hamlet* was actually on a ship off the coast of West Africa.

Shakespeare's litigious nature and eye for a business opportunity both feature in the book, while the bizarre stories of how the Bard's home was nearly demolished by the circus impresario P.T. Barnum and why his chair was vandalised by two future Presidents of the United States also make a welcome appearance.

His far-reaching cultural impact is highlighted by the odd tale of the Klingon version of *Hamlet* while his enduring ability to capture the imagination of people from all walks of life is brought into focus by accounts of the admiration he inspired in both Nelson Mandela and a certain Adolf Hitler.

There is also the truly surreal story of one of the most ambitious reimagining of any of his famous works, *King Lear with Sheep*.

The Bard's literary canon is unrivalled and the stories behind the plays he penned are as intriguing as the dramas themselves, revealing a man as colourful as the characters he created.

Shakespeare's Strangest Tales is a whimsical but loving tribute to the world's greatest writer and essential reading for anyone who has even briefly been dazzled by the brilliance of the Bard.

Iain Spragg

JOHN'S DREAM JOB

1557

William Shakespeare, we can all surely agree, is Stratford-upon-Avon's favourite and most famous son. Over the years the town has been home to, among others, science fiction heavyweight Arthur C. Clarke, promiscuous MP John Profumo and even shouty chef Gordon Ramsay, but the Bard remains Stratford's undisputed numero uno boy.

But before our Will was even a glint in his eye, and before he had put Stratford forever on the map with his quill, it was his father John who was making something of a name for himself in the area and we shall begin this book with the intriguing tale of how Shakespeare Senior landed himself arguably the greatest job in the world.

John Shakespeare was born in the small Warwickshire village of Snitterfield around 1530, the son of a humble tenant farmer, but a life in wellies was not for him and he relocated to Stratford to escape the stench of manure and seek his fortune. It proved a wise move and as his glove making and leather businesses in the town flourished, he was soon able to afford two houses, a new Volvo and regular holidays in the Algarve. Probably. He was, in short, making money hand over fist.

As such an upstanding citizen, it was not long before John was thrust into public office, first serving as an alderman and latterly a term as the chief magistrate of the town council. In 1557 however he got the plum gig as Stratford-upon-Avon's official beer taster.

It almost goes without saying that official beer taster ranks below only England football captain and lingerie consultant to Scarlett Johansson in the canon of dream jobs for men but it was, in truth, an important role.

'In 1557, about the time John Shakespeare married, he became ale-taster or "conner"', wrote Russell A. Fraser in his book *Shakespeare*. 'The local court leet, held by the manor lord to hear complaints of false measure, instructed him to fix the price of ale. He saw to it "that all brewers do brew good and wholesome ale and beer." Tasting this, he determined the "assize" or top price per gallon. Then a wooden hand went up before the alewife's house, beckoning for custom. First, though, the taster had to give his approval.'

Every town had a conner to ensure drinkers were not ripped off (or potentially poisoned) and although John was never subject to an official performance review, the records suggest the flow of good-quality beer in Stratford continued during his tenure. Everyone was hopelessly legless of a Saturday night at least, so he evidently ticked all the right boxes.

It would be seven years until William was born (more of which very shortly), and by that time John had reluctantly passed on the beer sampling mantle to another, but it seems pretty clear father and son discussed the role at some point judging by a passage in one of his subsequent plays.

'In *The Taming of the Shrew*, Sly, drunk on "sheer" or pure ale, rails on Marian Hacket, "the fat alewife of Wincot", a hamlet near Stratford,' wrote Fraser. 'Real-life Hackets lived there. This one poured to her patrons from earthenware jugs, "no sealed quarts" stamped by the conner, and Sly vowed to have her up before the leet.'

For reasons historians have never been able to shed satisfactory light on, John's rapid rise up the ranks of

Stratford society rather hit the skids in his later life and he fell into debt, perhaps after getting involved in illegal and ill-advised money lending. William helped his old man out whenever he could but poor John never quite recovered from the shock of having to actually pay for his beer again.

HAPPY BIRTHDAY, WILLIAM

1564

Historians adore Shakespeare. Some appreciate the timeless, sweeping themes he explores in his work, his breathtaking ability to analyse the human condition and lay bare universal truths. The vast majority however are fans because the Bard pays the mortgage.

Take a trip to your nearest Waterstones (other major book retailers are available), ask to be directed to the Shakespeare section and feast your eyes on the shelves festooned with weighty tomes on the life and times of our Will. You'd need a Ford Transit (once again, other vehicles are available) to get that lot home.

The proliferation of Shakespeare titles is chiefly due to the fact we know so little about the man and if there's one thing that historians love more than a big fat advance from a publisher, it's a subject open to interpretation and a well-penned theory or two. Wherever there's a lack of facts, there's always a historian poised to fill in the blanks. In hardback. A snip at £19.99 a copy.

Shakespeare has always been such an enigma. There are vast swathes of his life about which we know frustratingly little and even his birthday is a bone of contention among scholars who are not averse to a lucrative academic argument.

The traditional date given for the Bard's joyous entry into the world is 23 April 1564. The thing is no one can be 100 per cent sure, and although we do know the birth was recorded in the baptismal register of the Holy Trinity parish church in Stratford-upon-Avon on 26 April, the rest is essentially guesswork.

The Book of Common Prayer tells us that children were expected to be baptised on the first Sunday after the delivery or on the next holy day. Whichever came first really. The problem is, as things stand, Will should have been baptised on the twenty-fifth.

'If Shakespeare was indeed born on Sunday, April 23, the next feast day would have been St Marks Day on the twenty-fifth,' wrote Dennis Kay in *Shakespeare: His Life, Work and Era*. 'There might well have been some cause, both reasonable and great or perhaps, as has been suggested, St Mark's Day was still held to be unlucky, as it had been before the Reformation, when altars and crucifixes used to be draped in black cloth, and when some claimed to see in the churchyard the spirits of those doomed to die in that year. But that does not help to explain the christening on the twenty-sixth.'

Those who doubt Will came into this world on the twenty-third also point out that it's all rather too 'convenient'. That date, after all, just happens to be St George's Day and the cynics contend that the birth of England's greatest writer, coinciding with the day of the nation's patron saint, is unlikely. That Shakespeare just happened to die on 23 April 1616, lending his life story a suspicious sense of symmetry, only heightens the naysayers' doubts.

There is also a degree of dissention among the ranks about *where* Shakespeare was born. It is generally accepted his mother, Mary Arden, went through the whole agonising business of childbirth at the family house on Henley Street in Stratford but, again, we have no concrete evidence to back this up.

All historians, however, can agree one thing – debating the minutiae of the Bard's life in print is exceedingly good for the bank balance.

A MARRIAGE OF INCONVENIENCE

1582

'Hasty marriage seldom proveth well'. The words of Gloucester in Act IV, Scene I of *Henry VI, Part III* and a rather apt point to consider when we explore the subject of Shakespeare's marriage to Anne Hathaway in 1582, an intriguing union, which has long been the subject of fierce speculation.

Was it a union made in heaven or hell? Did William only embark on a career in theatre so he had an excuse to bugger off to London and escape her incessant nagging? Did he commit the cardinal sin and repeatedly leave the toilet seat up?

These are all valid questions but the one we really need to ask is whether the Bard actually wanted to marry Anne in the first place.

The couple tied the knot in November. Will was just 18 at the time, while Anne was 26 or 27 and, rather scandalously, she was already pregnant with their first child, Shakespeare's daughter Susanna. The vicar pretended not to notice the bump and with the nuptials hastily completed, the newlyweds settled down to family life.

The mystery of whether Anne was the Bard's first choice as Mrs Shakespeare however emerges when we look at an entry in the Episcopal Register of Worcester for 27 November, which reads '*item eodem supradicto die similes emanavit licencia inter Willielmum Shaxpere et Annam Whateley de*

Temple Grafton'. What do you mean you don't read Latin? OK, rough translation, 'and on the same day a [marriage] licence was also given between William Shaxpere and Anne Whateley of Temple Grafton'.

Who the hell is Anne Whateley? The plot thickens when we peruse a document in the same Worcester register, filed the following day, which dramatically reinstates Hathaway as Shakespeare's intended.

'The condition of this obligation is such that if hereafter there shall not appear any lawful let or impediment by reason of any precontract, consanguinity, affinity or by any other lawful means whatsoever,' it reads, 'but that William Shagspere on the one party and Anne Hathwey of Stratford in the diocese of Worcester, maiden, may lawfully solemnize matrimony together, and in the same afterwards remain and continue like man and wife according unto the laws.'

Certain scholars have argued this discrepancy in the documents is proof Shakespeare never wanted to get hitched to Hathaway. He was, they insist, the victim of a shotgun wedding, forced by his potential in-laws to abandon his true love Whateley, when news got out he was intending to do the dishonourable thing and leave the pregnant Anne in the lurch. The opposite camp is adamant it was merely a clerical error and whoever was responsible for updating the register simply spelt the name incorrectly the first time.

The matrimonial debate has raged for years but took a slightly implausible twist in 1939 when author William Ross published a book entitled *The Story of Anne Whateley and William Shaxpere as revealed by 'The Sonnets to Mr. W.H.' and other Elizabethan Poetry*, in which he claimed Whateley did exist and was actually responsible for writing all of Shakespeare's sonnets and many of the plays. He also maintained she wrote some of the poems attributed to Edmund Spenser, Christopher Marlowe and Sir Walter Raleigh, so we can probably pop him in the 'mad as a box of frogs' category of literary criticism.

A footnote to all this matrimonial mystery is that we don't know where William and Anne said their vows either. At the last count four churches – All Saints in Billesley, Temple Grafton, Luddington and Holy Trinity in Stratford-upon-Avon – had laid an opportunistic claim to being the venue for their nuptials, but not for the first time, it's all speculation.

Whatever the reality of Shakespeare's relationship with Hathaway and what exactly happened in the build-up to their 'hasty marriage', they were together for 34 years and produced three children. And, as far as we know, not once did they have to call on the services of the Stratford-upon-Avon branch of Relate.

FAMILY MISFORTUNES

1583

Treason is a recurrent theme in Shakespeare's work. His plays are positively teeming with dark and bloody tales of dynastic plots, monarchical machinations and attempted regicide and it appears the Bard may have taken some literary inspiration from real-life events rather disquietingly close to home.

Will's mother Mary Arden came from what we'd call a 'good' family. Her father was a landed farmer and pretty respectable but it is her distant cousin, Edward Arden, who concerns us here and who met with a grisly fate that would not have looked out of place in one of Shakespeare's own dramatic offerings.

Arden had the obligatory big pile in the countryside. He was the head of a noble family and he had a few bob. Unfortunately for him he was also a closet Catholic and in the reign of Elizabeth I and the febrile political and religious climate that accompanied her long stint as monarch, it was distinctly risky business to be a follower of Rome.

To compound his problems, Arden retained the services of a Catholic priest at the family home, masquerading as a gardener, and it was this clandestine cleric who effectively radicalised Arden's son-in-law John Somerville and sealed Edward's fate. Somerville vowed to kill his Protestant Queen, who he viewed as the tormentor-in-chief of his religion, and set off for London to assassinate her.

He was apprehended long before he got anywhere near Elizabeth. He was put on the rack and after a few judicious turns of the wheel by the mandatory bloke in a black hood, the squealer brought down the whole house of cards and gave up Arden, the priest (Father Hall) and Mrs Arden. The wrath of the Queen was both swift and brutal.

'On December 20, 1583, Edward Arden of Park Hall, the head of the Arden family in Warwickshire and a distant relative of Mary Arden Shakespeare, was executed for treason,' wrote Kate Pogue in her book *Shakespeare's Family*. 'Everyone in Stratford would have known about, gossiped about, discussed, and analysed this horrifying scandal.'

'The accused were indicted in nearby Warwick, tried in London, and on this grim December day Arden was taken from his prison cell, hanged, drawn, and quartered and his head posted on a pike on London Bridge. Father Hall disappeared and was perhaps murdered; Somerville was found strangled in his cell on the day he was to be executed; the lone survivor, Arden's wife Mary, was kept in prison then released several months later.'

Our Will was just 19 when all this occurred but he was fully aware of the family connection to the disgraced and subsequently decapitated Arden. It is hard to imagine such an event did not influence his work, not least his penchant for penning bloody and painful demises for so many of his characters. He was very much the Quentin Tarantino of his day.

Incidentally, there wasn't a shred of evidence against Arden beyond his son-in-law's confession under duress and he went to his gruesome death vehemently maintaining his innocence, claiming his only crime was to be a Catholic. His protestations were of course to no avail but he did at least dine on a fine last meal of ye olde fishye and chippes before he got the chop. Perhaps.

WILL GOES AWOL

1585

It is jolly difficult to disappear these days. You only have to caress a mobile phone, look the wrong way at a cash machine or spend five minutes in the same room as a laptop and you'll have left an inedible electronic trail that will betray your location to anyone who may be looking for you.

The proliferation of CCTV is another significant obstacle if you wish to vanish for reasons legitimate or otherwise (we're not judging here, although it is beginning to sound a bit dodgy), while number plate recognition technology means you're probably not going to get too far on the roads. In short, Big Brother and his minions know exactly where you are.

Things of course were different in Shakespeare's era, and whether intentionally or not, Will fell off the radar for seven years and between 1585 and 1592, and save for a brief mention in court papers regarding a land dispute heard in 1589 at the Queen's Bench in Westminster, we do not have a single documented reference to him. Not a single scrap of parchment with his name on. Not one solitary deed, receipt, letter or correspondence. He didn't even update his Facebook page.

The 'Lost Years', as they are imaginatively labelled, have sparked a veritable tsunami of theories about what Will was up to. His name appears in the papers referencing the baptism of his twins Hamnet and Judith in February 1585, and he is referred to obliquely in late 1592 in a pamphlet of literary criticism (more of which shortly), but the missing seven years between are a smorgasbord of historical hypothesis. And total guesswork.

The seventeenth-century author John Aubrey argued he worked as a country schoolmaster. The lawyer John Dowdall contended Shakespeare became a butcher's apprentice. In the early eighteenth century another theory had it that Shakespeare decamped to London to kick-start his theatrical career and made a living minding the horses of the capital's theatregoers. Others believed he buggered off to Europe and drank Chianti in Italy.

In his book *Sergeant Shakespeare*, published in 1949, Duff Cooper put forward the theory that William had either volunteered or been drafted into the army during the Armada crisis of 1588, citing the familiarity revealed in his later work with the lives of soldiers and military matters. There was even a suggestion in the 1950s that Shakespeare went to sea with Sir Francis Drake on the *Golden Hind*, but that does rather overlook the small fact the ship returned from its famous circumnavigation of the globe five years *before* Will went missing.

The mystery of the 'Lost Years' endures to this day and what the hell William was up to before he resurfaced in London in 1592 is worthy of an Agatha Christie novel. 'Abducted by aliens' is an increasingly popular modern explanation for Shakespeare's vanishing act but David Icke and his acolytes are of course mental (allegedly).

A SWING AND A MISS

1589

Whether it is by luck or sheer, unadulterated talent, certain practitioners of their particular trade enjoy immediate success. The legendary W.G. Grace, for example, hit a century on his Test debut for England against the Australians back in 1880, while Harper Lee certainly made her mark at the first time of asking in 1960, when she wrote *To Kill a Mockingbird*. The teenage chanteuse Britney Spears had a global chart topper with her first release '… Baby One More Time' in 1999 but that, admittedly, might have been a ghastly aberration.

Instant success is not though guaranteed for even the brightest stars in the firmament, and while we can safely celebrate the majority of Shakespeare's literary canon, his first attempt at penning a play was it seems something of a dramatic dud.

The ghost at the feast is *The Two Gentlemen of Verona*. Most scholars accept it to be the first of his plays, written sometime between 1589 and 1592, and when such esteemed titles as *The Oxford Shakespeare: The Complete Works* and *The Norton Shakespeare* place it as his earliest dramatic offering, who are we to argue.

Set in sixteenth-century Italy, it focuses on the story of two firm friends who become romantic rivals for the love of a noblewoman. It explores themes that he would expand on in later works but even now, more than 400 years later, no one has ever really taken to Will's first stab at being a playwright.

The American literary critic, Harold Bloom, dismissed it as 'the weakest of all Shakespeare's comedies'. Professor Harold Clarke Goddard declared it 'contains some of the most boring wit', while even Isaac Asimov was so disappointed after reading *The Two Gentlemen of Verona* he speculated whether 'the version we now have is a mangled copy of the real play'. Not glowing endorsements then.

It is not just those esteemed gentlemen who have failed to embrace the work and it remains one of the least staged of all Shakespeare's plays. The earliest documented staging was in 1762 when it was heavily rewritten by theatre impresario Benjamin Victor, but the production closed after six performances, while a 1784 reincarnation in Covent Garden survived for just one night despite being originally scheduled to run for several weeks.

It has been adapted for British television only twice, compared to the countless screen versions enjoyed by its dramatic cousins, and the only straight cinematic retelling of the story was released in China in 1931. As a silent movie. Pretty poor when you consider that, in 1999, the *Guinness Book of Records* listed a grand total of 410 feature-length films and television versions of Shakespeare's plays.

Will of course got significantly better at the whole playwriting business but the distinctly lukewarm reception enjoyed by *The Two Gentlemen of Verona* does illustrate that even the undisputed greats need time to hone their talents.

But wait, breaking news. There is one tale of *The Two Gentlemen of Verona* enjoying significant success in the world of entertainment. It was a rock musical on Broadway between 1971 and 1973 that ran for 614 performances and won a coveted Tony Award for Best Musical. Just when you thought the Bard had bombed.

CRITICAL ASS

1592

It was on New Year's Day 1962 that a young popular beat combo by the name of The Beatles pitched up at a recording studio in North London to audition for Decca Records. The lads from Liverpool did their thing and waited to hear whether they had landed their big break in the shape of a juicy recording contract.

A few weeks later Decca famously told John, Paul, George and Pete (Ringo would turn up later) that the band had 'no future in show business' and decided instead to sign Brian Poole and the Tremeloes (who subsequently mustered a grand total of one solitary UK chart topper). It proved of course to be one of the greatest misjudgements in the history of pop music, eclipsing even Posh Spice's attempt to launch a solo career or the UK's recent entries in the *Eurovision Song Contest*.

Decca's disastrous dismissal of The Beatles however looks like a minor error in critical judgement in comparison to the man who wrote the first ever review of Shakespeare's work nearly 400 years earlier, an appraisal of the Bard's talent which, retrospectively, must have left the man in question wondering what the hell he was thinking. If he wasn't already dead.

Our misguided reviewer is theatre critic Robert Greene. His initial opinion of Shakespeare was committed to paper in his 1592 pamphlet entitled *Groats-worth of Witte, bought with a million of Repentance,* and he's evidently not a big fan of the Bard.

'There is an upstart Crow,' he wrote, 'beautified with our feathers, that with his Tygers hart wrapt in a Players hyde, supposes he is as well able to bombast out a blanke verse as the best of you: and being an absolute Johannes fac totum, is in his owne conceit the onely Shake-scene in a country.'

OK, so it's slightly cryptic but stick with it. 'Upstart crow' is a clear insult, which academics believe is a reference to Shakespeare's lack of university education. 'Tiger's heart wrapped in a Player's hide' alludes to a line in *Henry VI, Part III*, while 'Shake-scene' is an obvious play on the Bard's name. Throw in the negativity of words like 'bombast' and 'conceit' and that 'Johannes fac totum' means 'Jack of all trades' and you have a literary two fingers up akin to a Simon Cowell put-down on *The X Factor*.

What so enraged Greene about Shakespeare remains something of a mystery. As well as indulging in criticism, he was a playwright himself and while the world of theatre and acting is obviously renowned for the absence of ego, petty jealousies and hissy fits, perhaps Greene was a tad jealous.

It is worth remembering that *Groats-worth* was published after Greene had shuffled off this mortal coil in September 1592 and some suspicious scholars contend that the surreptitious quill of another writer or writers was at work on the pamphlet post mortem.

What we do know for sure is that his first, negative review hardly crushed Shakespeare's confidence or creativity and he successfully penned some half-decent stuff in the years that followed Greene's tirade from the grave.

THE UNTAMED SHREW

1596

Nimbys are an oft-derided group. Those who object to having a nuclear-powered waste-recycling plant complete with an adjacent open-air abattoir located a few yards from their front door are frequently dismissed (by those a comfortable distance from the aforementioned carbuncle) as selfish and oblivious to the wishes of the wider community. 'It's got to go somewhere', the man from the council in the cheap suit and luminous yellow jacket invariably protests.

The 'Not in my Back Yard' movement is far from a new phenomenon, as Shakespeare and his pals discovered in 1596, when they inadvertently incurred the displeasure of a lady who made Margaret Thatcher look like a pushover.

For reasons that shall become clearer later (see 'Relocation, Relocation, Relocation, 1599'), the Bard and his cohorts were on the lookout for a potential venue to stage their dramatic endeavours. A theatre in Blackfriars had just been built and, hey presto, negotiations began about the possibility of Will's work being staged at the new playhouse.

Step forward Elizabeth Russell, the self-styled dowager countess of Bedford, a resident of Blackfriars and a woman evidently to be reckoned with. An educated lady who had been married twice, Elizabeth wore a widow's hood that contemporary accounts said made her look like a cobra poised to strike and she had a fearsome reputation for getting exactly what she wanted.

In 1590, for example, she became the first woman in the country to own a castle. Rumours abounded she acquired her piece of prime real estate through bribery and she was infamous for settling land disputes with her neighbours by kidnapping, forgery and, on occasion, having men hung by their heels to make them see the error of their ways. Definitely no 'weak and feeble woman' then.

When she heard a troupe of unruly actors might be moving in next door, she sprung into action and did what all self-respecting Nimbys do in times of crisis, she organised a petition. She wasn't having hordes of theatregoers shattering her peace at all hours of the day and night and, as a committed Puritan, she was desperate to ensure services at the nearby church of St Anne's were not disturbed by all that thespian nonsense.

Elizabeth quickly strong-armed 30 of Blackfriars' finest into signing and the pressure grew to stop the theatre opening for business. If Shakespeare was annoyed at the countess' intervention, he must have been bloody furious when he saw two of the names on her petition, none other than his own patron Lord Hunsdon and his publisher Richard Field, a fellow Stratford lad, but the damage had been done and plans to relocate to Blackfriars were abandoned.

'She derailed Shakespeare's career, but only temporarily,' wrote Frances Wilson in the *New Statesman*. 'He avenged himself sending up her kinsmen in *Henry IV* and *The Merry Wives of Windsor* and immortalising her son, Thomas Posthumous Hoby, as the Puritanical Malvolio in *Twelfth Night*. Several scenes from her life are encrypted in his plays and Elizabeth's final appearance in Shakespeare is as the dowager Countess of Rousillon in *All's Well That Ends Well.*'

Will's literary comeback was perhaps lost on Elizabeth, who was obviously not an avid theatregoer herself, but his audiences probably got the joke. A victory for Russell then? Let's call it a score draw.

THE TAXMAN COMETH

1598

The image of the impoverished artist is a romantic one that has resonated for decades. A creative fat cat is all wrong and it was the nineteenth-century German painter Carl Spitzweg who rather poignantly captured the whole 'suffering for one's art' vibe when he produced *The Poor Poet*, a work which depicts a down-at-heel writer surrounded by books in a shabby garret, an umbrella above the bed to tackle a leaking roof.

It would be tempting to picture Shakespeare in such a threadbare light, a struggling playwright more concerned about polishing the wording of Hamlet's soliloquy than his bank balance, but our Will was far from the breadline. In fact, the Bard was absolutely rolling in it.

The evidence is damning. According to a study conducted by Aberystwyth University in 2013, Shakespeare was hauled before the courts for grain hoarding and was repeatedly threatened with prison for tax evasion. Scandalous indeed but proof William was an astute businessman who was rather successful at feathering his nest when he wasn't busy with his quill.

'There was another side to Shakespeare besides the brilliant playwright, as a ruthless businessman who did all he could to avoid taxes, maximise profits at others' expense and exploit the vulnerable while also writing plays about their plight to entertain them,' said Dr Jayne Archer, a lecturer in medieval and renaissance literature and the lead researcher of the study.

'It's one of the things that we've forgotten about Shakespeare. As well as writing for people who were experiencing hunger, he was exploiting that need himself. He was using his role as a playwright and the public playhouses, gathering coin, in order to take advantage of the market when it's at its most profitable and selling food at inflated prices to secure the long-term future for his family. Remembering Shakespeare as a man of hunger makes him much more human, much more understandable, much more complex.'

'In February 1598 he was prosecuted for holding 80 bushels of malt or corn during a time of shortage. He pursued those who could not pay him in full for these staples and used the profits to further his own money-lending activities. Profits were channelled into land purchases. He also acquired tithes on local produce, including corn, grain and hay, allowing him to cream off the profits from others' manual work.'

Crikey, he makes Gordon Gekko look like Mother Teresa.

Shakespeare however was apparently far from ashamed of his dubious dealings and they shed new light on his play *Coriolanus*, which was written around the same time as a peasant revolt in the Midlands in 1607, an angry uprising in protest at artificial food shortages created by the wealthy elite, and a work which was initially interpreted as a dramatised defence of the plight of the poor and hungry.

'They ne'er cared for us yet: suffer us to famish, and their store-houses crammed with grain,' bemoans the 'First Citizen' in a scene from Act I of *Coriolanus*. But when we consider Will's own brush with the law for grain hoarding, the play becomes less a moral treatise on inequality and exploitation, and rather more a brazen and barefaced theatrical biopic.

We perhaps should not condemn the Bard for his financial

acumen, but had there been a seventeenth-century version of *Dragons' Den*, Shakespeare would have been the one seated comfortably in his chair, smugly stroking piles of silver, rather than sweating profusely as he desperately pitched for cash in return for a 20 per cent share in his 'Quills'R'Us' business.

RELOCATION, RELOCATION, RELOCATION

1599

Shakespeare was being a little disingenuous when he wrote 'All the world's a stage' in *As You Like It*. No Will, stages are almost exclusively found inside things called 'theatres'. It's where actors do acting, audiences assemble and you can buy exorbitantly overpriced little tubs of ice cream.

The Globe Theatre is the venue with which the world associates the Bard. The original building is long gone but the story of why Shakespeare's plays were famously brought to life on its boards rather than a rival theatre is worth retelling.

Before the 1570s London did not boast a single purpose-built playhouse. Acting companies performed in inns, colleges and private houses, but that all changed in 1576, when actor and agent James Burbage raised sufficient funds to build a shiny new theatrical structure in Shoreditch. After days of agonising about the name, Burbage apparently gave up and decided to call it the 'Theatre'. Four years later Shakespeare joined Burbage's troupe (later known as the Chamberlain's and then the King's Men) and the Bard was officially in the business.

In 1596, however, a dispute began between the company and the landowner over the renewal of the Theatre's lease. The row rumbled on rancorously for three years and by the end of 1598, Shakespeare and his chums had finally had enough and decided a change of scenery (pardon the pun) was what was required. Their brush with Elizabeth Russell (see 'The Untamed Shrew, 1596') had put the kibosh on a possible move to Blackfriars and it was time for a new approach.

'In Christmas 1598 the company sought a drastic solution,' relates the *Shakespeare's Globe* website. 'They leased a plot near the Rose, a rival theatre in Southwark, demolished the Theatre and carried its timbers over the river. To cover the cost of the new playhouse, James Burbage's sons, Cuthbert and Richard, offered some members of the company shares in the building. Shakespeare was one of four actors who bought a share in the new venture. By early 1599 the theatre was up and running and for 14 years it thrived, presenting many of Shakespeare's greatest plays.'

The intriguing element of this tale is to what extent Will got his hands literally and metaphorically dirty in the relocation. Did he put writing *Much Ado About Nothing* on hold, grab the nearest piece of four by eight and lug it across the Thames? Maybe he was responsible for unscrewing the doors to the Theatre's dressing rooms and hauling them down to Southwark. Or perhaps he was more of your hands-off, foreman type.

Whatever the extent of his manual labour (or lack of it) the Theatre was shifted and, resplendent in its new surroundings, it was renamed The Globe.

Unfortunately Shakespeare and Co. neglected to install fire alarms and in 1613 The Globe was razed to the ground by flames caused by the shooting of a theatrical cannon on stage during a performance of *Henry VIII*.

'Now, King Henry making a masque at the Cardinal Wolsey's house,' wrote Sir Henry Wotton in a letter to his nephew after witnessing the event, 'and certain chambers being shot off at his entry, some of the paper or other stuff, wherewith one of them was stopped, did light on the thatch, where being thought at first idle smoke … it kindled inwardly, and ran around like a train, consuming within less than an hour the whole house to the very grounds. Only one man had his breeches set fire, that would perhaps have broiled him, if he had not by the benefit of a provident wit put it out with a bottle.'

The theatre was promptly rebuilt, but the second incarnation of the venue survived for only 31 years, and in 1644 under pressure from the Puritan movement, who maintained it was a den of iniquity and generally a bit too bawdy for their tastes, it was demolished. Party people the Puritans were not. Or, evidently, fans of the theatre.

EXIT KEMPE, STAGE LEFT

1599

It is invariably a reflection of the quality of the performance when an actor becomes synonymous with a certain role. For many, for example, Sean Connery is the quintessential Bond, Ian McKellen the living embodiment of Sherlock Holmes, and while the slightly salacious debate that rages over whether Michelle Pfeiffer or Halle Berry was the definitive Catwoman may never be satisfactorily resolved, actors yearn to really nail a part in the public's eye.

Back in Shakespeare's day, the go-to thespian for all your comic and clownish theatrical requirements was an actor called William Kempe and he was by all accounts a veritable hoot. 'He was a big man who specialized in Plebian clowns who spoke in earthly language,' wrote Charles Boyce in his *Shakespeare A to Z*. 'Kempe's characters have a tendency to confuse and mispronounce their words, and contemporary references to his dancing and ability to "make a scurvy face" suggest a physical brand of humour.'

Kempe joined James Burbage's Chamberlain's Men in 1594 and subsequently played, among other characters, Dogberry in *Much Ado About Nothing*, Bottom in *A Midsummer's Night Dream* and Lancelot Gobbo in *The Merchant of Venice*. It was though in his portly portrayal of the famed Falstaff in the Bard's two *Henry IV* plays that he really hit his straps and audiences lapped it up.

Around 1598, however, Kempe quit the company in what

appear to be acrimonious circumstances and, shortly afterwards, Shakespeare had a bit of a problem. He was writing his big sequel, aka *Henry V*, and with no Kempe on hand to bring life to Falstaff once again, he was faced with a dramatic quandary.

Will came up with a novel solution and rather than recast another actor in the part, he simply killed Falstaff off. Off stage. 'My manly heart doth yearn,' says Pistol in Act II, Scene III. 'Bardolph, be blithe: Nym, rouse thy vaunting veins: Boy, bristle thy courage up; for Falstaff he is dead, and we must yearn therefore.' The cause of his abrupt theatrical death is said to be a broken heart caused by his rejection by the King.

It's a neat trick by Shakespeare but let's now return to the circumstances of Kempe's mysterious departure from the troupe. We cannot be certain why he left but there is a theory he was essentially fired because of his penchant for improvisation. The Bard did not like actors mangling his words and a speech in *Hamlet* certainly suggests Shakespeare had an axe to grind. 'And let those that play your clowns speak no more than is set down for them,' our eponymous antihero says in Act III, Scene II. 'For there be of them that will themselves laugh, to set on some quantity of barren spectators to laugh too.'

Ever the entertainer, Kempe attempted to maintain his profile by embarking on a bizarre journey in 1600, Morris dancing 100 miles (161km) from London to Norwich, but while he did continue to act, his post-Shakespearean career hit the skids and he appears to have died in poverty in London in 1603. Whether he had the proverbial last laugh before shuffling off this mortal coil is debatable.

FREEDOM OF THE PRESSES

1599

Imitation may indeed be the sincerest form of flattery but there is a distinct difference between paying homage through affectionate mimicry and simply half-inching somebody's work without so much as a by your leave. Or a royalties cheque. Or even a thank-you card with a few kisses at the bottom.

Copyright infringement is severely dealt with these days. Hordes of voracious lawyers – possibly barracked in secret underground lairs and fed on raw meat – are poised to spring into action should anyone be foolish enough to violate their clients' intellectual property and 'borrow' one too many of their *bon mots*.

The history of copyright law began in 1710 with the British Statute of Anne. Or, to give it its full title, deep breath now, 'An Act for the Encouragement of Learning, by vesting the Copies of Printed Books in the Authors or purchasers of such Copies, during the Times therein mentioned.' It was the first time it became illegal to reprint a book without permission.

Shakespeare though lived and wrote in less regulated times, and suffice it to say, the seventeenth century was the publishing equivalent of the Wild West.

The first man to rip off the Bard was one William Jaggard, a leading printer and publisher in London. Jaggard was, it appears, always on the lookout for a moneymaking opportunity and with Shakespeare's star on the rise, he decided there was an appetite for his work. In 1599 *The Passionate Pilgrim by W. Shakespeare* hit the shelves and by all accounts Jaggard did his bank balance no harm whatsoever in the process.

The book contained a few of Will's sonnets, some taken from *Love's Labour Lost*, as well as poems by other writers but which Jaggard erroneously attributed to the Bard. He didn't even text Shakespeare to seek permission but the law being what it was, he essentially got away with his flagrant breach of copyright.

The poets who had their odes printed under Shakespeare's name were livid and one, Thomas Heywood, made it abundantly clear in a letter to a friend that Will was very much 'not on board' with Jaggard's little project.

'I must necessarily insert a manifest injury done me in that worke,' he wrote, 'by taking the two Epistles of Paris to Helen, and Helen to Paris, and printing them in a less volume, under the name of another (Shakspeare), which may put the world in opinion I might steale them from him; and he; to doe himself right, hath since published them in his own name: but as I must acknowledge my lines not worthy his patronage under whom he hath publish them, so the author (Shakspeare) I know much offended with M. Jaggard that (altogether unknowne to him) presumed to make so bold with his name.'

Perhaps emboldened by the success of *The Passionate Pilgrim*, Jaggard was at it again in 1619 when he published what has become known as the *False Folio*, a reprint of earlier versions of ten plays including *King Lear*, *The Merchant of Venice* and *Henry V*, purported to have been penned by Shakespeare but which actually included dramatic works that had absolutely no connection to our Will.

The Statute of Anne of course was yet to be enacted, but there were still some rules about reprinting work belonging to the King's Men; Jaggard circumvented all that silly legal nonsense by changing the dates on the original folios he was working from. In layman's terms, he fiddled the paperwork. Shakespeare would have been incandescent had he not died three years earlier.

Remember William Jaggard's name, however, as our pickpocket of a publisher will make two further appearances in the pages that follow ...

PLAYING WITH POLITICS

1601

We have previously explored how Shakespeare's relative Edward Arden got himself rather brutally executed after a failed bid to topple Queen Elizabeth I (see 'Family Misfortunes, 1583') but in this tantalising tale of politics and plotting, it is our Will himself who comes perilously close to the chop.

The central figure in our story, however, is Robert Devereux, the second Earl of Essex. The year is 1601 and after enjoying significant influence at the royal court, Devereux suddenly found himself in the Queen's bad books after leading a lacklustre military foray over in Ireland that spectacularly failed to subdue the locals. His ignominious return to Blighty left Liz, who had ordered him to stay put until the job was finished, seething.

The Earl was a worried chap. He could count the dwindling number of his important friends on one hand and, in a blind panic, hatched a plot to oust Elizabeth and her senior advisors in a popular uprising. It was very much a case of getting his retaliation in first.

The plan was to incite the good folk of London to rise up with Essex against the court but Devereux decided that he needed to sow the seeds of sedition in the capital before making his audacious move. A little stirring of the pot was what was required.

Enter Shakespeare and the King's Men, who were

approached by the Earl's representatives and asked to stage a special performance of *Richard II* at The Globe. Unsurprisingly they were asked not to spare the horses when the time came for the scene in which Richard is dethroned. The messengers promised there was 40 shillings in it for them and Will and his fellow actors duly obliged with a rendition of the treasonous play.

Two days later Essex marched into London with a small band of supporters but the tidal wave of popular support he was banking on failed to materialise. He was subsequently imprisoned, subjected to the very definition of a show trial and unceremoniously denied the ongoing use of his head after the swing of the executioner's axe at the Tower of London.

The papers from his trial made it crystal clear that the Crown was well aware what Devereux had been up to when he requested the Bard and Co. to stage their special performance.

'The official documents of the case tell their own story,' wrote Peter Ackroyd in *Shakespeare: The Biography*. '"The Erle of Essex is charged with high Treason, namely That he plotted and practised with the Pope and king of Spaine for the disposing and settling to himself Aswell the Crowne of England, as of the kingdome of Ireland." In one count of the indictment he was charged with "permitting of that most treasonous booke of Henry the fourth to be printed and published ... also the Erle himself being so often present at the playing thereof, and with great applause giving countenance and lyking to the same." The treasonous book was John Hayward's account of the abdication and murder of Richard II. The drama that the Earl of Essex greeted with great applause was Shakespeare's play of the same name.'

Whether the King's Men were aware of Essex's intentions or plot is pure conjecture but, whether unwittingly or not, Shakespeare had got himself associated with a traitor. Elizabeth was not exactly reluctant to sanction a beheading or ten and his life expectancy must have dipped sharply as events unfolded but she mercifully did not give the order. The King's Men breathed a collective sigh of relief while Will quietly ditched plans for his new play entitled *The Queen Must Die*. Which, incidentally, she did two years later.

THE SECRET SEDUCTION

1602

Shakespeare's plays abound with tales of bedroom-related tomfoolery, amorous action and, you know, general sexual shenanigans. The Bard was definitely no literary prude and while his characters were not exclusively motivated by getting their leg over, sex does play a rather prominent part in much of what he wrote.

Such a proliferation of erogenous activity in his dramas has prompted much speculation over the years whether Will had sex on the brain and was in fact a 'bit of a lad' himself. Of course we know he remained married to Anne Hathaway until his dying day, but let's face it, he would have been far from the first (or last) famous married man to have succumbed to temptation.

Suggestions that Will was indeed unfaithful to Anne emerged in 2016 when the British Library staged a new exhibition to commemorate the four-hundredth anniversary of the Bard's death entitled 'Shakespeare in Ten Acts' and an intriguing story of how Will reportedly enjoyed his wicked way with a female theatregoer was revealed.

The source for our saucy tale is the diaries of a chap called John Manningham, a seventeenth-century law student and friend of Shakespeare. The amorous assignation took place in March 1602 and, according to Manningham, it went something like this.

The Bard's great actor chum Richard Burbage was playing

the lead role in *Richard III* in London. A lady in the audience was so taken with his performance that she approached Burbage after the show and invited him to her place later on so that they might, ahem, become 'better acquainted'. Burbage was instructed to use the code name Richard III on his arrival so that his female fan would know her beau was at the door.

Unbeknownst to Burbage, however, Shakespeare had overheard the pair arranging their booty call. Will decided to gatecrash the party, arriving at the house earlier than his theatrical friend and, according to Manningham's diaries, having used the agreed code name to cross the threshold, he 'was entertained and at his game' with the lady in question. To compound Burbage's understandable frustration, the Bard then sent his fellow actor a note proclaiming, 'William the Conqueror was before Richard III.' The cheeky little devil.

'John Manningham did have mutual friends with Shakespeare – such as Ben Jonson and John Donne – so there are links between the two men', Tanya Kirk, the exhibition curator, told *The Daily Telegraph*. 'The anecdote was obviously the talk of the town at the time and it fits nicely in with the picture we have of Shakespeare being a witty person. His note to Burbage is brilliant – it could be something out of one of his comedies. There is so little evidence about what Shakespeare was like as a person, so things like this take on huge significance.'

Will may well have thought himself quite the wag after taunting Burbage but he probably wouldn't have been laughing had the angry actor written to Anne to fill her in on exactly what her errant hubby had been getting up to in the Big Smoke.

SHOW ME THE MONEY

1604

Neither a borrower nor a lender be,
For loan oft loses both itself and friend,
And borrowing dulls the edge of husbandry.

Polonius, *Hamlet*, Act I, Scene III

Wise words there from Polonius. His financial acumen may have failed to impress the Prince of Denmark himself, Hamlet dismissing him as a 'tedious old fool' before stabbing him, albeit accidentally, to death, but in our age of instant credit, payday loans and record levels of bankruptcy, the old fella made a pertinent and timeless point.

It would be tempting to assume Shakespeare shared similar views on matters of the coin. He wrote the lines for Polonius after all but it seems the Bard was a chap who was not averse to lending money from time to time.

We know this from court papers dating back to 1604 when Will felt compelled to seek legal redress against one Philip Rogers. Our Phil had apparently agreed to buy 20 bushels of malt from Will at a cost of 39 shillings and ten pennies, but in an unfortunate case of short arms and deep pockets, he had only coughed up a measly four shillings. Shakespeare wasn't happy, hence the court appearance, and made a claim for the outstanding balance plus ten shillings in damages. Crucially he also asked for the repayment of a further two shillings he had loaned to Rogers.

There's sadly no record of the court's judgement. Most historians assume Rogers stumped up because there's no further documented mention of the dispute, and the Bard was nothing if not tenacious, and would have been unlikely to let the matter slide if payment had not been forthcoming. But even if he did win the case, the fact it all ended up in an unedifying legal wrangle does rather underline Polonius' original point that no good can come from lending.

Interestingly Shakespeare was back in the same Stratford court four years later when a local fella by the name of John Addenbrooke also incurred his financial ire. He was evidently a litigious bugger and this time the Bard sued for the recovery of six shillings. To be fair, that would buy him a hell of a lot of quills and ink.

It's unclear whether the sum was a loan or unpaid business debt, but Will once again was not prepared to let

it drop, and although the dispute dragged on for ten long months he continued to press for repayment. Addenbrooke was arrested and then bailed, when local blacksmith-cum-landlord Thomas Hornby came forward to stand as surety for him, but Addenbrooke promptly did a Shergar and Lord Lucan all rolled into one and disappeared.

Like a monetary Rottweiler, Shakespeare then insisted Hornby pay the debt and the court ruled in his favour, ordering Stratford's purveyor of fine ales to cross Will's palm with the six shillings and 24 more in damages. Even Wonga doesn't charge that kind of rate of interest.

There's no evidence whether Hornby actually produced the readies but the whole business certainly sealed the Bard's reputation as an individual who was 'careful with money'. Rumours that Will was in fact born in Yorkshire rather than Stratford began to circulate shortly afterwards.

AN EXPLOSIVE SITUATION

1605

The phrase 'light the blue touch paper and stand well back' is one familiar to all those who've held a box of fireworks on Bonfire Night, anticipating the pyrotechnic display to follow, but also hoping to avoid getting their fingers burned. It can be a dangerous business playing with fire.

Bonfire Night is of course a quintessentially British way of celebrating the foiling of Guy Fawkes' dastardly plan to blow up the Houses of Parliament in 1605. Mr Fawkes suffered more than a set of singed digits for his role in the notorious plot, executed as he was for treason, but it seems that a certain William Shakespeare was rather fearful of suffering a similar fate. Fawkes ultimately failed to light the blue touch paper but it was the Bard who was standing well back in the aftermath of the event.

Let's be clear about this, the Bard was not involved in the Gunpowder Plot. He didn't even help police with their enquiries and, if anyone asks, he was in Ye Olde Eel and Codpiece having a quiet pint. He did though have connections to the Catholic conspirators, who'd had it up to the back teeth with Protestant persecution, and what they saw as the oppressive reign of James I.

Will's father John was friends with William Catesby, whose son Robert was up to his neck in it with Fawkes. Moreover the Bard's favourite boozer was the Mermaid Tavern in London, which just happened to also be the preferred watering hole for the conspirators as they finalised their plan of attack. It wasn't, on balance, looking particularly good for Will should the long arm of the law put two and two together, come up with five, and feel his collar.

The burning question was how to distance himself from the whole unfortunate business. A simple letter of denial might have looked a tad suspicious, and being the dramatic genius that he was, many literary historians believe Will simply picked up his quill and proceeded to scribble himself out of potential trouble.

James I was Scottish and not long after the Gunpowder Plot was foiled, Shakespeare began work on *Macbeth*, his first and only Scottish play. Coincidence? Hardly. The Bard was on a serious charm offensive and the King would have his ego stroked.

'Change after change was made until the play became a perfect propaganda machine that seemed to clear Shakespeare of any suspicion,' wrote Amanda Mabillard on *Shakespeare Online*. 'James' favourite part of Shakespeare's new take on history would be the near mythological qualities given to the character created in his image – Macbeth's victim, King Duncan. While the real Duncan was a war-loving Neanderthal, Shakespeare's Duncan is a thoughtful, infallible, divinely-appointed ruler with "silver skin" and "golden blood."'

'Shakespeare wove direct references to the Gunpowder Plot right into *Macbeth*. To commemorate the discovery of the heinous scheme, King James had a medal created picturing a snake hiding amongst flowers. Lo and behold, we find a nod to the medal right in the play when Lady Macbeth tells her husband to "look like the innocent flower, but be the serpent under it".'

The Bard went even further. One of the plotters, Father Garnet, confessed his involvement after initially denying any knowledge of the conspiracy and earned the moniker the great 'equivocator' after claiming he lied for God's sake.

'Here's an equivocator,' says Macbeth's porter in the play, 'that could swear in both the scales against either scale; who committed treason enough for God's sake, yet could not equivocate to heaven. O, come in, equivocator.'

The PR offensive worked a treat. The Bard was not bundled into the back of a black Maria in the middle of the night and *Macbeth* was a big hit in royal circles and beyond, proving that while the pen may indeed be mightier than the sword, it's also frightfully adept in the right hand at averting the finger of suspicion.

FEWER WORDS FOR THE FAIRER SEX

1606

'Shakespeare has no heroes,' observed Samuel Johnson in 1765, 'his scenes are occupied only with men.' The good Doctor was referencing the moral ambiguity of so many of the Bard's leading characters when he wrote that line, but at the same time, Johnson, albeit unwittingly, rather shone a light on Will's rampant misogyny.

OK, that's a bit strong. Shakespeare didn't hate women. He married one after all and his plays are populated by a host of strong female characters that boast real depth and complexity. The Bard might even have been in touch with his feelings for all we know and it's worth noting that he comes out of Germaine Greer's book, *Shakespeare's Wife,* relatively unscathed.

The point here is that Will didn't exactly give his women equal dramatic billing. Seen but not heard would be an exaggeration, but if we take *Antony and Cleopatra* as our template, written in 1606, and first performed the following year, it does seem he favoured the male voice.

According to the seminal work on the number of words uttered by Shakespearean characters, Marvin Spevack's 1974 *Concordance,* the Queen of Egypt speaks 4,686 words during the course of the play. Old Antony gets 5,949, which means he has 25.1 per cent of the total dialogue, compared to 19.7 per cent for the lovely Cleo.

Not exactly an equal share then and the picture of a

playwright reluctant to let the women get a word in worsens when we take a wider look at the Shakespeare canon. Of the 20 most verbose characters in all the plays, only one is a lady. Cleopatra limps in at twenty-first in the chart, and it is left to Rosalind to speak up for the women with her 5,698 words in *As You Like It*, placing her eleventh on the list. Sisters might be doing it for themselves but in Shakespeare they're doing it quietly.

Even Juliet has to play second fiddle to her lover boy. She has 4,271 words compared to 4,677 delivered by Romeo. The tortured soul that is Hamlet has the most to say in Shakespeare, enunciating a tongue-twisting 11,563 words.

Those who are having none of these accusations that Will was a touch sexist would argue that it's quality not quantity that matters and cite *Macbeth*, conceding that while the title character has 715 lines compared to just 259 from Lady Macbeth, her 'presence' in the play is just as prevalent as that of her husband.

Whether you believe the Bard let the female side down in his work is ultimately a matter of opinion. And probably depends on whether your ideal weekend involves beer and watching sport or having your nails done followed by a glass of Pinot Grigio.

Before we move on, however, let's go back to our meticulous friend Mr Spevack, whose surgical dissection of the Bard also reveals that *Antony and Cleopatra* features the shortest speaking part of any named character in all of his plays. Our chap is called Taurus, he appears in Act III, Scene VIII, and his entire verbal contribution is to ask 'My Lord?' before keeping schtum for the rest of proceedings. Unsurprisingly it's not a role that actors who've spent three years studying at RADA flock to audition for.

HAMLET ALL AT SEA

1607

If you were to ask, in the style of the oddly enduring television quiz show *Family Fortunes*, 100 people to name Shakespeare's most famous play, *Hamlet* would surely be the most popular answer. The work is a cultural phenomenon and although it's not exactly a laugh a minute, it has conquered the world with performances in over 75 different languages and more productions over the years than any of its envious dramatic cousins.

The early performance history of the work, however, is as vague as the titular character's psychiatrist's bill must have been hefty. We believe the Bard penned his seminal work sometime between 1599 and 1602, we think he always had his old chum Richard Burbage of the King's Men in mind to play the Prince of Denmark and we think that the play was staged not long after Will's ink had dried on the parchment. There are even unproven tales of Shakespeare himself playing the Ghost in early productions.

This though is all conjecture, albeit relatively educated, and we must venture far from London's theatre land and beyond the dramatic venues of the provinces to uncover the first documented performance of *Hamlet* in 1607.

The scene is the Atlantic Ocean. More specifically, we are off the coast of Sierra Leone, West Africa, on the deck of the imposing *Red Dragon*, a former Royal Navy cruiser now operated by the East India Company. Ship and crew are going nowhere due to a conspicuous lack of wind and the skipper, Captain William Keeling, is racking his brains how best to entertain the chaps.

He eschewed a shuffleboard tournament. A swimming gala was suggested and promptly rejected based on the number of sharks circling the boat and Keeling eventually decided to offer up a cultural diversion to pass the time.

'I invited Captain Hawkins [from sister ship the *Hector*] to a ffishe dinner,' he wrote in his diary, 'and had Hamlet acted abord me which I permit to keepe my people from idleness and unlawful games or sleepe.'

It's intriguing that Keeling had a copy of the play on hand in the first place but more tantalising is how the roles were allocated. It's easy to imagine a slew of volunteers for Hamlet or Laertes, not least because of the sword fight scene, but you'd have to pity the poor sod press-ganged into playing Ophelia, knowing full well, as he reluctantly donned a dress for the big production, that he'd be the butt of the entire ship's jokes for the rest of the voyage.

THE SEA VENTURE'S MISADVENTURE

1609

The Bard, we can safely assume, was quite the history buff. Will's work is awash with historical inspiration and from *Antony and Cleopatra* to *Richard III*, *Julius Caesar* to *King John*, Shakespeare was never averse to plundering the past for a dramatic premise or three.

He was though also a keen observer of contemporary events in the seventeenth century, and in *The Tempest* we have a rare example of the Bard turning to current affairs as the thematic backdrop for one of his plays. The idea probably came to him after watching the News at Ten.

Set on a remote island, *The Tempest* of course tells the tale of the shipwreck of the usurper Antonio after his brother Prospero, the rightful but deposed and exiled Duke of Milan, conjures up a storm to force his sibling onto his mystical atoll. It's a fantastical start to the play and one which you could be forgiven for believing Will created with that big brain of his.

The reality however, seems to be rather more prosaic when we explore the real-life tale of the shipwreck of an English vessel by the name of the *Sea Venture* on Bermuda in 1609, just two years before the Bard is believed to have written *The Tempest*.

The *Sea Venture* was the flagship of a fleet of nine boats carrying 500 bright-eyed colonists from Blighty to America. *En route* from the Canary Islands to Virginia however, the fleet was enveloped by a hurricane of Biblical proportions, which wreaked all kinds of nautical havoc, and the *Sea Venture* was presumed lost at sea when it failed to turn up in Jamestown, the capital of Virginia.

It had in fact become 'fast lodged and locked' between coral boulders just off the coast of the uninhabited Bermuda and all 150 passengers and crew, including the skipper Sir George Somers and Virginia's new governor Sir Thomas Gates, had managed to safely get to *terra firma* on the ship's row boats.

The whole tempestuous event was preserved for prosperity in the letters of William Strachey, one of the passengers who eventually made it to America on one of two makeshift vessels nine months later. 'A dreadful storm and hideous began to blow from out the Northeast', he wrote, 'which swelling, and roaring as it were by fits, some hours with more violence than others, at length did beat all light from heaven; which like an hell of darkness turned black upon us, so much the more fuller of horror, as in such cases horror and fear use to overrun the troubled, and overmastered senses of all, which (taken up with amazement) the ears lay so sensible to the terrible cries, and murmurs of the winds, and distraction of our Company, as who was most armed, and best prepared, was not a little shaken. For surely as death comes not so sudden nor apparent, so he comes not so elvish and painful (to men especially even then in health and perfect habitudes of body) as at Sea.'

Strachey's description is certainly redolent of the scene painted by the Bard at the start of *The Tempest* as Antonio's ship is thrown against the rocks, and although there is no documentary proof that Shakespeare based the drama on the fate of the *Sea Venture*, the relatively brief gap between the real wreck and Will's dramatic version strongly suggests he did indeed 'borrow' elements of the headline-grabbing story. Literary critics also argue the tale of Prospero, Caliban and Ariel is a metaphor for the fractious relationship between English colonists, slaves and the indigenous people of the New World.

One thing we can be sure of is the Bermudan Tourist Board is absolutely convinced the Bard was inspired by the story of the *Sea Venture*, and should you be fortunate enough to take a trip to the island today you can stay at the Ariel Sands Beach Club, quench your thirst at Caliban's Bar and then party the night away at Prospero's Cave. Just make sure you fly to the island rather than taking the boat.

BIZARRE
BIBLE STUDIES
1611

The world loves a good conspiracy theory. How else can we explain how *The X-Files* ran for nine seasons, 202 episodes and spawned two motion pictures? Or why some persist in believing that Elvis Presley faked his own death and is currently enjoying his dotage away from the public eye, quietly growing kumquats, perhaps in Guatemala?

There is, of course, no shortage of 'interesting' theories about the Bard. The really big one is the perpetual argument over who wrote 'his' plays, which we shall come to later, but for now we shall focus on religion, birthdays and hidden messages that would have kept Alan Turing and his fellow boffins at Bletchley Park interested for at least an hour. Or maybe 30 minutes tops.

The source for our tale is the King James Bible which, guess what, was published on the orders of King James I. The work took seven long years to complete, as the country's finest scholars pored over the original Latin text and painstakingly translated it into English, and in 1611 it was ready to hit the shelves. And churches obviously.

Except for priests and their congregations, nobody gave it much more serious thought until 1900, when an article appeared in *The Publishers' Circular* that claimed that a close study of Psalm 46 revealed a rather intriguing anomaly. The forty-sixth word from the start of the psalm is 'Shake' ('the earth doth *shake*') while the forty-sixth word from the end is 'spear' ('God cutteth forth a *spear*'). If we assume that he was 46 when the King James Bible was printed, we suddenly have a cryptic birthday message dedicated to the Bard.

If the Internet had been invented in 1900, the forums would have gone into meltdown at news of the revelation. It wasn't, but that didn't dampen the fevered levels of speculation about how the secret anniversary annotation got there.

One school of thought was that Shakespeare himself was one of the scholars charged with delivering the new Bible, and when no one was looking, he had deliberately manipulated the translation of Psalm 46 to include his little in-joke. A secret signature, if you like.

Others contend that Will had no direct involvement with the project and that Lancelot Andrewes, Bishop of Winchester, a man famed for his verbal dexterity, was responsible for encoding the message at the behest of Francis Bacon. The joke here being that Bacon is the man some insist wrote all of Shakespeare's plays but, once again, that is for another time.

Sceptical academics have dismissed the Psalm 46 revelation as nothing more than pure coincidence, and have pointed out that if you take the first letter from the first word of each paragraph, it spells out 'I shot JFK'.

WILL'S ERRANT QUILL

1612

The advent of chip and PIN technology in the UK in 2004 was a revolution in banking. For the first time cashiers were spared the excruciating task of matching an incomprehensible scrawl on the till receipt to the signature on the back of a debit card.

Shoppers no longer had to worry about payment being declined because suspicious store workers thought they were faking it, and although it's been a nightmare for those who struggle to remember those all-important but elusive four digits, the system has been an overall success.

Shakespeare would have been a chip and PIN man. His era was of course very much cash orientated, but had he been required to carry plastic for all those day-to-day transactions down Stratford High Street, the Bard would have been banged up for fraud just moments after enquiring whether he could borrow a pen.

The problem was his signature. We have only six surviving examples of his autograph deemed authentic, but the variations in his scrawl and spelling suggest that while he was very mindful of his penmanship when writing his plays, he had a rather more indifferent attitude to making his mark.

The earliest signature we have from him comes from legal papers from 1612, a case in which Will was a witness in a dowry dispute, where he signs his name 'Willm Shakp'.

In 1613 he was in the process of buying a property in Blackfriars in London, and in the conveyancing paperwork he writes 'Wm Shakspe', only to pen 'Willm Shaksper' in the subsequent mortgage documents.

The three other examples come from his last will and testament. On both the first and second sheets of the will the Bard scribbles 'Willm Shakspere', finally achieving a brief degree of consistency, but on the third sheet he goes off piste again and writes 'William Shakspeare'.

In his defence, there were no standard spelling rules in his day. It was very much a free-for-all with words transcribed as they sounded, but for a man who earned his living as a writer, it is still surprising Shakespeare didn't appear to know how to spell his own name. Or at least settle on one version that took his fancy and persevere with it.

On the basis of the Bard's shocking inability to get his own name right, it will probably come as little surprise that there are over 80 variations of the spelling of 'Shakespeare' from contemporary documents, diaries and essays.

The literary world continued to play fast and loose with his name right up to the mid-twentieth century. In 1913, for example, Brander Matthews wrote a book entitled *Shakspere as a Playwright*, and in 1947 T.W. Baldwin's *Shakspere's Five-Act Structure* was released but the 'Shakespeare' camp, spearheaded by academics from the University of Cambridge, was already on the march and today all but the most dyslexic modern scholars accept the 11-letter variation.

AN IMPERFECT PARTNERSHIP

1613

The phrase 'two heads are better than one' was first recorded in John Heywood's *A dialogue conteinyng the nomber in effect of all the prouerbes in the Englishe tongue*, published in 1546, and it's an adage that did the careers of such distinguished pairings as Lennon and McCartney, Benny and Björn, and Rodgers and Hammerstein no harm whatsoever. After all, why do all the work yourself when you can share the load a little?

Literary cooperation is as well established as writing duos are in the music business and even the great Bard himself was not averse to pulling up an extra chair and getting down to work with another author. We may think of him as a solitary, standalone genius but Shakespeare did in fact have a partner in crime.

His name was John Fletcher and although history has been kinder to the Bard, he was one of the most celebrated, prolific and popular playwrights of the era. In short, Fletcher was hot stuff, and in very much the same way that McCartney's pairing with Stevie Wonder for *Ebony and Ivory* in 1982, or David Bowie's collaboration with Mick Jagger three years later on *Dancing in the Street*, were seen as dream tickets, any dramatic mash-up between John and Will was surely a theatrical hit just waiting to happen.

It didn't exactly go according to plan. They first shared writing duties on what has become known as a 'lost play' called *Cardenio*. They renewed their partnership in 1612 to produce *Henry VIII* but it is Shakespeare's thirty-sixth and last-ever play, *The Two Noble Kinsmen*, and Fletcher's role in it that is our focus here.

Written in 1613, its plot is taken from 'The Knight's Tale' in Chaucer's *The Canterbury Tales* and set in Athens, but like *Henry VIII* before it, critics generally accept it's not the finest example of Shakespeare's work. It's not awful, they argue, but it lacks the zing of previous offerings. Samuel Pepys described it as 'no excellent play' while modern productions are at best sporadic.

A slightly disappointing note to end the Bard's career on then, but perhaps not all that disappointing when we examine just how much of the work can be attributed to our Will, rather than Fletcher. Shakespeare's hand is undeniably all over the drama but it seems he played a supporting rather than lead role.

'There is still basic agreement about the attribution of many of the scenes,' wrote Lois Potter in the Arden edition of the play. 'Everyone gives Shakespeare the whole of Act 1, the prose scene that opens Act 2, and most of Act 5, the exceptions being, possibly, the first seventeen lines of scene 1 and, more certainly, 5.2, which ends the story of the Jailer's Daughter. On the other hand, no one thinks him responsible for the scene in which the young men first see Emilia or for the one in which they reminisce about the women in their lives.'

'There still remains, however, considerable disagreement how much the two writers collaborated on the subplot. It is often said to be entirely Fletcher's, once Shakespeare has introduced the characters in 2.1, but some scholars give Shakespeare the Daughter's soliloquy in 3.2 and the first scene with the Doctor in 4.3.'

Disagreement or not, that makes Fletcher the dominant pen in proceedings, outscoring Shakespeare three acts to two. It might be churlish to suggest Fletcher's contribution to the play is the reason for its lukewarm critical reception but let's just say the Bard didn't have these problems when he sat down all on his lonesome to pen *King Lear* or *Romeo and Juliet*.

The play did make a brief and unexpected cameo appearance in an episode of *The Simpsons* first broadcast in 2004, when bartender Moe gives away a rare bottle of 1886 Chateau Latour. To compound his misery, he then wipes his tears on an original manuscript of *The Two Noble Kinsmen*.

IMMOVABLE IN DEATH

1616

Nobody knows what killed Shakespeare on 23 April 1616. We can be fairly sure it wasn't the sniper on the grassy knoll, but exactly what did precipitate the demise of the English language's greatest writer is a mystery that will probably never be solved.

John Ward, the vicar of Holy Trinity Church in Stratford, where Shakespeare is buried, wrote in his diary 50 years after his death that 'Shakespeare, Drayton, and Ben Jonson had a merry meeting and it seems drank too hard, for Shakespeare died of a fever there contracted', while C. Martin Mitchell, the biographer of the Bard's son-in-law, argued 'that it was more likely than not in the nature of a cerebral haemorrhage or apoplexy that quickly deepened and soon became fatal.' In an age when the average life expectancy was around 40, it's equally conceivable that the 52-year-old had simply had his time.

Whatever did prompt Will to shuffle off this mortal coil, it seems he still had enough time to scribble down his own epitaph for his gravestone. It endures to this day and it reveals a man who was rather preoccupied with being disturbed in the afterlife:

Good friend for Jesus' sake forbear,
To dig the dust enclosed here:
Blest be the man that spares these stones,
And curst be he that moves my bones.

To be fair to Shakespeare he wasn't being paranoid, as graves were frequently dug up in the seventeenth century and bodies exhumed to make room for new burials, but Will's poetic warning did the trick and he remains exactly where he was first laid to rest, unmolested by the living.

The same however cannot be said of his funerary monument, located inside Holy Trinity, a limestone likeness of the great man, which has been subjected to redecoration, redesign and even wanton vandalism, since it was commissioned to celebrate his life and work.

We do not know exactly when the monument was carved, but scholars agree it was *in situ* inside the church by 1623 at the latest, and since it was installed it has been repainted numerous times, most notably in 1793, when fêted Shakespearean scholar, Edmund Malone, persuaded the vicar it would look just right in all white. In 1861 the white was expunged and the original colours recreated.

More dramatically, the monument underwent a rather major overhaul in 1747, when the good folk of Stratford decided that the first design of Shakespeare holding a bag of grain, nodding to his mercantile exploits, rather missed the whole 'literary genius' vibe they wanted to achieve and it was rehewn to depict the Bard holding a pen. The fact the original design did rather look like Will was clutching the bag suggestively to his groin had absolutely nothing to do with the radical makeover.

The pen survived sometime into the eighteenth century but someone, a clumsy parishioner dusting the church perhaps, snapped it off and ever since a real goose quill has stood in its place to ensure we don't forget our Will was a writer. Shakespeare. Literature. Got it?

The monument suffered its greatest indignity in 1973 when burglars broke into the church and chipped the stone bust away from its setting. Police believed they were looking for original Shakespearean manuscripts, rumoured to be hidden inside the monument, but the thieves left empty handed and fortunately the figure suffered only superficial damage.

It's well worth a trip to Holy Trinity to see the grave and monument for yourself, but under no circumstances pack a feather duster, chisel or live goose.

THE GREAT BED DEBATE

1616

It is highly advisable to write a will before you cash in your chips and join the choir invisible. Leaving your estate intestate is a recipe for disaster and should you not make your post mortem wishes crystal clear, it's inevitable Auntie Marjorie and Cousin Cybil will come to unseemly blows over who gets their grubby, avaricious mitts on your priceless antique grandfather clock.

Shakespeare made no such mistake before he checked out. The Bard was a pragmatic man and everything was absolutely in order after his death. His eldest daughter Susanna got his property portfolio, his other daughter Judith received £100 with more cash to follow and even the poor of Stratford got a mention, with Will bequeathing them £10.

But what about the missus? What did he leave his wife Anne Hathaway? You may remember that some scholars contend the pair did not enjoy the happiest of unions (see 'A Marriage of Inconvenience, 1582') and judging by the Bard's will, they might have a point. 'I give unto my wife,' it reads, 'my second best bed with the furniture.'

Talk about two fingers from beyond the grave. A measly bed? The girls get houses and cash and Anne gets a bed. It's even more desultory when you realise 'the furniture' isn't even furniture in the sense of a nice mahogany sideboard, or an attractive walnut cocktail cabinet, but actually the bedding and pillows. She got an old bed and some second-hand sheets.

'Among the very few facts of his life that have been transmitted to us, there is none more clearly proved than the unhappiness of his marriage,' wrote Charles Knight in *William Shakespeare, A biography*. 'The dates of the births of his children, compared with that of his removal from Stratford, the total omission of his wife's name in the first draft of his will, and the bitter sarcasm of the bequest by which he remembers her afterwards, all prove beyond a doubt both his separation from the lady early in life, and his unfriendly feeling towards her at the close of it.'

So more Charles and Diana then as opposed to Wills and Kate.

But things might not be quite as they first seem. Although it's true there are no terms of endearment towards Anne in the wording of the will, neither are there any affectionate *bon mots* directed to his daughters and while there is no financial provision stipulated, historians point out that as his widow, Anne would have automatically been entitled to a third of his estate and to live in the family home in Stratford until her own death.

And then we come to the 'second best bed', which would have been in fact the marital bed. The 'best bed' in those days was reserved for visitors, and it's perfectly plausible to argue that the bequest of 'their' bed to Anne, was actually a loving nod and wink from beyond the grave.

'If we may suppose that some provision had been made for her during his lifetime,' wrote James Boswell in the early nineteenth century, 'the bequest of his second best bed was probably considered in those days neither as uncommon or reproachful.'

The debate about the meaning of the Bard's bequest and what it tells us about the true state of his marriage rumbles on and, in the absence of a hitherto undiscovered stash of love letters to Anne, there will always be cynics who maintain Mrs Shakespeare was more of a matrimonial mistake than muse in the story of our Will.

PRESERVED FOR
PROSPERITY IN PRINT

1623

Hindsight may be a wonderful thing, but here it is foresight which interests us, and the debt owed to a pair of gentlemen by the names of John Heminges and Henry Condell, erstwhile thespian colleagues of Shakespeare, and a duo who were chiefly responsible for ensuring much of the Bard's work was not lost forever.

The dilemma was, with Will in the grave, 18 of his plays survived only in rough, hand-written form, and there were alarmingly few copies knocking about. An inopportune fire, an opportunistic burglary or even a particularly voracious book worm (or whatever creepy-crawly it is that actually eats paper) could have halved the Shakespearean canon overnight and Heminges and Condell were determined that wasn't going to happen on their watch.

They decided that what was rather urgently required was a printed collection of all Shakespeare's work, both the previously typeset plays and those that only existed in draft form, including big-hitters *The Tempest*, *Macbeth*, *Antony and Cleopatra* and *The Comedy of Errors*, and so the project, which was to become known as the 'First Folio', began.

It was the first time anyone had attempted to bring together the Bard's 36 dramas inside one cover and, as well as ensuring his genius would be preserved for prosperity, the pair wanted to ensure lesser talents could no longer mangle his words and plots as they had done in previous single reprints of his plays. They were, in their own words, vehemently opposed to the 'stol'n and surreptitious copies, maimed and deformed by frauds and stealths of injurious impostors.' They would present the Bard's works 'offer'd to your view cured, and perfect of their limbes; and all the rest, absolute in their numbers as he conceived them.'

The pair of course needed a printer to help deliver their literary rescue mission and here comes the twist in this tale, because one of the two members of the Stationers' Company they approached for the gig was William Jaggard, the man who had twice unashamedly ripped the Bard off by publishing his work without permission (see 'Freedom of the Presses, 1599').

As long-standing members of the King's Men, Heminges and Condell must have been fully aware of Jaggard's nefarious previous activities in relation to their late chum, and their decision to involve him in the project initially seems odd.

It was though an era in which printing was a highly specialised business and Jaggard was one of the few, if not only, men in town who had the kit and caboodle required to handle the volume of work Heminges and Condell were proposing. Pragmatism won over whatever sense of resentment they were harbouring and, no doubt reassured by the fact by now Jaggard Senior was infirm and blind and much of the day-to-day business of the company was looked after by his son Isaac, they gave the firm the job.

The First Folio hit the shelves in London in December 1623. An estimated 800 copies were churned out by Jaggard Junior in the first print run and each one cost one pound, which is roughly equivalent to £170 in today's money. You had to pay extra to get your book bound in leather mind, and the first recorded customer for the new title was one Sir Edward Dering, who really splashed out and treated himself to two copies.

Heminges and Condell's work was done. Whether they made any real money themselves from the venture is unknown but the cultural legacy they secured is absolutely priceless.

There are two appendices to our story. The first is that William Jaggard popped his clogs a month before the First Folio went on sale, which means this time he was unable to profit from Shakespeare's name.

The second is, and whisper it quietly now, one of the most seminal books in the entire history of the English language was actually printed on paper imported from, the shame, France. The problem was that the embryonic English paper industry wasn't ready to supply the volume of quality of parchment needed and the high-end rag paper required had to be shipped from across the Channel. This inconvenient truth is why UKIP have vowed to remove any reference to the First Folio from the National Curriculum when they sweep to power at the General Election in 2020.

LOST AND FOUND

1653

Bookish types are not usually known for their fiery tempers or propensity to anger quickly, but if you should want to cause a riot at any given literary gathering, simply raise the question, with a disingenuous smile, as to exactly how many plays Shakespeare wrote. A wag once did just that at the Hay Festival and half the Powys constabulary had to be drafted in to sort out the resulting brouhaha.

Most scholars, but even then by no means all, accept the Bard penned 37 plays, albeit some with varying degrees of collaboration with other writers. Beyond that it's academic anarchy with some suggesting he was responsible for up to five more dramatic works, taking the total to 42, while others cry heresy at such dangerous talk.

The play, one of Will's disputed 'five', which is the subject of this discussion is titled *Cardenio*. It's a play believed to have been based on an episode in *Don Quixote* involving the character of Cardenio, and one which has a chequered and fascinating history, which ultimately ends in redemption and, fingers crossed, no further fisticuffs among our learned friends.

We must start in 1613, when records from the royal annals reveal *Cardenio* was first performed in London, but there is no mention of the identity of the author. Nothing more was heard of this enigmatic work until 1653, when a prominent London publisher by the name of Humphrey Moseley made an entry in the Register of the Stationers' Company that he intended to publish *Cardenio* and attributed the work jointly to our Will and his previous collaborator John Fletcher.

Mystery solved? Sadly not, because Mr Moseley somewhat impinged his own credibility when he wrongly registered plays called *Henry I* and *Henry II* as the Bard's and given that he'd also tried, three years earlier, to pass off works entitled *The History of King Stephen*, *Duke Humphrey, a Tragedy* and *Iphis and Iantha, or A Marriage Without a Man, a Comedy*, as being from the same quill. The sceptics were, well, sceptical, and nobody gave Moseley's claims that Will wrote *Cardenio* the time of day.

It was all quiet on the Western Front for the next 74 years, but in 1727 the English playwright Lewis Theobald claimed to have unearthed three Restoration-era manuscripts of an unnamed play by the Bard. The industrious Lewis edited and 'improved' the scripts he had secured and duly published them under the title *Double Falsehood*. The killer point here is that *Double Falsehood* has the same plot as the Cardenio episode in Don Quixote. Spooky or what?

Initially Theobald got the same treatment as Moseley before him as the naysayers, including literary heavyweights such as Alexander Pope, dismissed his 'Shakespeare manuscripts' as forgeries. It didn't help his cause that they were mysteriously destroyed in a library fire so that no one could verify their authenticity.

That might have been the end of the story but his claims were cast in a different light when subsequent generations realised that evidence of Moseley's 1653 registry entry was only revealed after Theobald had died. In short, he knew nothing about it, and people began to reassess the possibility that Theo's much derided manuscripts really were copies of Shakespeare's *Cardenio*.

The lobby to anoint the play as a genuine Bard work has been growing in strength, and in 2010 Gary Taylor, the editor of the New Oxford Shakespeare and professor of English at Florida State University, published the results of 20 years of research on the *Double Falsehood* using lots of clever computer world analysis wizardry and old-fashioned document cross-checking, and came to the conclusion it was indeed based on something originally penned by Shakespeare.

'The first thing you have to do is identify what bits come from the eighteenth century and get rid of those,' he said. 'Increasingly, with the availability of massive databases and more sophisticated attribution tests, the consensus is now that it's partly by Shakespeare and partly by Fletcher. But the eighteenth century text we have is seriously messed with and modified.'

So there you have it, the Bard wrote at least *38* plays. It may though be prudent to keep that information to yourself at certain bookish events lest the presence of the boys in blue be required.

DON'T MENTION THE 'M' WORD

1672

Did you know that the Ouija board gained widespread popularity in the West when it was marketed as an innocent parlour game by an American entrepreneur back in 1890? Fun for all the family was the general gist of Elijah Bond's sales spiel and it is only in the intervening years that the boards have gained their association with the occult and communicating with the dead.

It is probably prudent though not to dabble in the dark arts and the supernatural unless you're properly qualified and have a HND from Hogwarts. As America learned after invading Vietnam, you just never know what you're messing with.

The Bard should perhaps have heeded this mantra when he wrote *Macbeth*. In particular, he should have been very mindful of what he committed to paper when he penned the famous witches' speech ('Double, double toil and trouble' *et al*) in Act IV, Scene I, because his literary flirtation with the dark side has caused all sorts of problems ever since.

Dear Will was so focused on imbuing the scene with realism that he actually used the incantations of real witches, proper spells and everything, and ever since successive generations of thespian types have been convinced the play is cursed. This is why actors religiously refer to the work only as the 'Scottish play' rather than *Macbeth*, and why the mere mention of the 'M' word is believed to invoke said curse, and a catalogue of unfortunate accidents on anyone associated with the production.

Superstitious poppycock? Perhaps, but the weight of evidence to suggest that being involved in a performance of *Macbeth* is more dangerous than, say, *A Midsummer Night's Dream*, cannot be dismissed. The 'Scottish play', it seems, can definitely be harmful to your health.

Written between 1599 and 1606, there are scant contemporary references to early performances, but legend does have it that on opening night Hal Berridge, the boy cast to play Lady Macbeth, died backstage and Shakespeare himself was hastily drafted in to play the future Queen. The tale is admittedly hearsay but nonetheless it's not exactly an auspicious start.

The first documented casualty connected to the play happened in 1672, in Amsterdam, when the actor playing the titular character stabbed to death the poor sod who'd been handed the Duncan role. On stage, right in front of the audience. Rumours the dead actor had been sleeping with the prop manager's wife were likely to have been slanderous but the unfortunate incident did rather cement *Macbeth*'s reputation as a poisoned dramatic chalice.

Since then tales of sometimes fatal misfortune have abounded. In Sir John Gielgud's production in 1942, three actors died and the set designer committed suicide, and in 1967 director Peter Hall contracted shingles and nearly went blind while overseeing his interpretation of the play at the Royal Shakespeare Theatre. As recently as 2013, a cast member was injured onstage and taken to hospital during Kenneth Branagh's *Macbeth* in Manchester.

There have been attempts to disentangle the play from the curse but it's a moot point how successful they have been. In 2001, for example, a group of white witches descended at the site of the old Inverness Castle where the drama is set in a bid to banish the attendant bad luck but things did not go smoothly.

Two witches didn't even turn up. One got spooked after her pet dog died, while the second refused to budge after her cat brought home a black feather. You'd have thought witches, white or otherwise, were made of sterner stuff. The eerie incidences didn't stop there though and during the ceremony a cameraman was rushed to hospital after suddenly falling ill, and a radio reporter, wait for it, inexplicably dropped his equipment. The pair had absolutely definitely not been spotted drinking together into the wee hours at the local hotel.

'I sensed a great power that just drained away all my energy,' said one of the witches. 'I remember feeling fear. I sensed a very, very evil spirit. I believe in this curse definitely now. If I did not before, I do now.'

It's inconclusive whether the 'Scottish play' was successfully exorcised that day, or whether the curse ever existed, but what we do know, without equivocation, is that should you meet an actor and wish for whatever reason to scare the living daylights out of them, you know exactly what to say.

HAPPILY EVER AFTER
1681

You could never accuse Shakespeare of lacking versatility. The Bard had a range bigger than the AGA catalogue and his dramatic works run the gamut from comedy, romance and history, right through to the darkness that pervades his tragedies. Will was Jack of all trades and master of the lot.

To quote the fifteenth-century monk, John Lydgate, however, you can't please all of the people all of the time, and a chap called Nahum Tate evidently had a bit of an issue with one specific area of the Shakespearean *oeuvre*. We're talking the tragedies here and in particular *King Lear*.

Tate's problem was his belief the play was a bit gloomy and depressing. All those deaths at the end and a royal family ripped asunder by politics, greed and jealousy, he thought was unnecessarily morose and wouldn't audiences prefer something a bit more jolly and upbeat? Tate duly took it upon himself to lighten the mood, and in 1681 he published *The History of King Lear*, a 'reworking' of Shakespeare's original.

Talk about chutzpah. In Tate's new offering, Lear does not die from a broken heart and instead reclaims his throne and lives to a ripe old age, contentedly shod in warm slippers, puffing on his pipe. Cordelia escapes execution by hanging in prison and instead marries Edgar and they buy a nice semi in St Albans. The other sisters – Goneril and Regan – desist from poisoning each other, are ultimately reconciled and go shoe shopping. In his own words, Tate had begun with 'a Heap of Jewels, unstrung and unpolisht; yet so dazling in their Disorder, that [he] soon perceiv'd [he] had seizd a Treasure' and proceeded to mutilate the Bard's plot.

The incredible thing is that his Disneyfied take on *Lear* was a big box office hit. Samuel Johnson certainly approved because he could not countenance Cordelia's death while the eighteenth-century critic Charles Gildon agreed the lower body count was to be applauded. 'The King and Cordelia ought by no means to have dy'd,' he wrote, 'and therefore Mr Tate has very justly alter'd that particular, which must disgust the Reader and Audience to have Vertue and Piety meet so unjust a Reward ... We rejoice at the deaths of the Bastard and the two Sisters, as of Monsters in Nature under whom the very Earth must groan. And we see with horror and Indignation the Death of the King, Cordelia and Kent.'

For the next 150 years or so Tate's abomination was almost exclusively the version of the play staged in theatres as sentimental audiences lapped up his Lear light, but by the mid-nineteenth century the worm began to turn, as critics savaged his saccharine monstrosity and 'Tatification' became a derogatory term for unnecessary interference.

'After surviving so many sufferings, Lear can only die,' wrote the German poet and celebrated Shakespeare translator August Schlegel. 'And what more truly tragic end for him than to die from grief for the death of Cordelia? And if he is also to be saved and to pass the remainder of his days in happiness, the whole loses its signification.'

It was the beginning of the end for *The History of King Lear*, and although there have been some ill-advised modern revivals, the play on the whole has been consigned to the 'what the hell were we thinking?' section of literary history. Mercifully Tate's plans to rewrite *Hamlet* and have the Prince of Denmark speak the lines 'To be or not to be, It's not really important, is it?' never came to fruition.

MEAT IS MURDER

1709

The Elizabethans adored a spot of venison. Deer was very much on the menu and contemporary chefs would go to great lengths to ensure the meat was as succulent as possible. 'Take [the venison] and lard it with Lard,' reads one Elizabethan recipe. 'And stick it thick with Rosemary, then roft it with a quick fire ... baste it with sweet butter: then take half a Pint of Claret wine, a little beaten Cinamon and Ginger, and as much sugar as will sweeten it, five or six whole Cloves, a little grated bread, and when it is boiled enough, put in a little sweet butter, a little Vinegar and a very little Salt. When you meat is rosted, serve it with Sauce.' Anyone else feeling peckish?

Shakespeare couldn't apparently resist a delicious dish of deer either and if we are to believe an early eighteenth-century account of the Bard's activities, he was even prepared to stoop to illegal means to get his hands on his meat of choice.

The source for our tale is the dramatist and poet Nicholas Rowe, who earned the distinction of becoming Shakespeare's first ever biographer, when he published *Some Account of the Life & c. of Mr. William Shakespear* in 1709. In his book Rowe asserts that sometime between 1585 and 1592, aka the 'Lost Years', young Will was caught poaching deer on the land of Sir Thomas Lucy at Charlecote Park, just 4 miles (6.4km) from his home in Stratford-upon-Avon.

Lucy was a well-connected chap with royal backing and, according to Rowe, Will was facing a bit of porridge for his misdemeanour and made himself scarce.

It's a colourful story but sadly we have no contemporary evidence to back it up. Some believe it's true and argue the Bard's need to suddenly split lest he end up in jail explains why the 'Lost Years' were, well, lost, while the sceptics argue he didn't even own a bow and arrow.

The incident, fictitious or not, did make an impression on subsequent generations and The Shakespeare Birthplace Trust Collection boasts a nineteenth-century oil painting by an unknown artist entitled 'The Deer-stealing Episode at Charlecote', while there is also an engraving from 1861, which shows our Will being brought before Lucy to answer for his crimes.

Legend also has it that the Bard exacted a characteristically poetic revenge on Sir Lucy, composing a scurrilous ballad about him before posting it on the gates of his Warwickshire estate. Again we have no documented record of this revenge rhyme, but Rowe does offer a version he claims had been preserved by word of mouth in the local area:

A parliamente member, a justice of the peace,
At home a poore scarecrow, at London an asse.
If lowsie is Lucy, as some volke miscalle it,
Then Lucy is lowsie whatever befalle it:
He thinkes himselfe greate,
Yet an asse in his state,
We allowe by his eares but with asses to mate.
If Lucy is lowsie, as some volke miscalle it,
Sing lowsie Lucy, whatever befalle it.

If Will's ode did indeed exist, Lucy would probably have choked on his venison when he read it.

NO PAIN, NO GAIN

1750s

It's tough to break into acting. Aspiring young thespians have to endure all kinds of indignities before they're able to make a living on stage, and whether it's a few hours a week working as a kids' entertainer, or a stint dressed up as a rooster, brandishing a placard advertising the culinary delights at the nearby 'Quick Chick' fried food emporium, the stars-in-waiting have to earn a crust. The really unlucky ones end up making cameos as injured teenager number three on *Casualty*.

The eighteenth-century thesp David Garrick knew all about the battle to make it big in theatre. A failed wine merchant, Garrick determined to tread the boards in the early 1750s and although his early performances suggested he did have a certain *je ne sais quoi* on stage, he wasn't exactly an overnight success.

That all changed however when he landed the titular role in Shakespeare's *Richard III*. He was, by all accounts, a veritable *tour de force* as the Bard's iconic Machiavellian monarch and he brought an intensity to the part which won over theatregoers and the literary elite alike. 'That young man never had his equal as an actor,' noted Alexander Pope, 'and he will never have a rival.'

And when we say intense, we mean intense. So much so in fact that there's a persistent, although potentially apocryphal, story that Garrick actually fractured his leg during a performance of *Richard III*, but was so immersed in his portrayal of the scheming lead character that he failed to notice his injury and carried on until his curtain call. Myth or not, many insist the tale is the origin of the phrase 'break a leg', that famed theatrical expression of good luck.

In Garrick's case, *his* broken leg certainly did bring him improved fortune. After his successful stint as Richard, he went on to play a series of high-profile roles to great acclaim and later in life went on to buy a share in, and then manage, the Theatre Royal in Drury Lane. Such was his social standing when he died in 1779, that he was afforded a lavish public funeral at Westminster Abbey, and laid to rest in Poets' Corner.

There is another interesting connection between Garrick and the Bard: the former staging the Shakespeare Jubilee in Stratford-upon-Avon to commemorate the 200th anniversary of the latter's birth. Considering the debt Garrick owed Shakespeare, it was undoubtedly a nice gesture but there were two major problems with the event, namely it was held in 1769, some *205* years after Will's birth, and not a single Shakespeare play was performed over the three days of festivities.

Garrick may well have been a fine actor but would, it appears, have struggled to properly organise a drinks party in a distillery.

GASTRELL'S ARCHITECTURAL GAFFE

1759

'When I was at home,' says the court jester Touchstone in Act II, Scene IV of *As You Like It*, 'I was in a better place.' He may have been a Fool but like all of his dramatic peers in Shakespeare, Touchstone had a way of hitting upon the truth. Whether Shakespeare shared his creation's devotion to the domestic is debatable but let's stick with the 'home' theme for now and explore the fate of the Bard's old house.

The gaff in question is New Place in Stratford-upon-Avon, which Will, flush with cash derived from his theatrical successes in London, bought in 1602, when he returned from the Big Smoke to his home town. It was, we are led to believe, the second best house in Stratford at the time and as soon as the ink was dry on the contracts, the Shakespeares moved in *en famille*.

We cannot be certain, but it's highly likely Will breathed his last in New Place in 1616, but after his death the property stayed in the family, through his daughter Susanna and granddaughter Elizabeth, until her death in 1670, when it passed into the ownership of her husband's family.

By 1753 however, the second best house in Stratford belonged to one Reverend Francis Gastrell, and this is when all the problems started. The first bone of contention was a mulberry tree in the gardens of New Place, which was said to have been planted by the Bard himself, and it attracted rather a lot of visitors eager to view it. The Gastrells quickly tired of all the looky-loos peering over their garden wall and Mrs Rev is said to have hacked it down in a fit of pique. The residents of Stratford were evidently unimpressed with this act of (horti)cultural vandalism and made their feelings clear by smashing a few of the Gastrells' windows.

But that was merely the *hors d'oeuvres* however, and when, three years later, Gastrell applied for planning permission to extend the aforementioned garden, he was summarily knocked back by local officials. To make matters worse, he was also involved in a tax dispute with the same council employees, and increasingly close to the edge. The untimely appearance of yet another 'Shakespeare tourist' ogling the house tipped him over and the Reverend promptly had New Place demolished.

Stratfordians were incandescent and ensured their unwelcome neighbour was made to feel even more unwelcome indeed. 'Gastrell quarrelled with the Corporation over the assessment of his monthly levy and eventually, in 1759, he razed New Place to the ground,' wrote Simon Andrew Stirling in his book, *Who Killed William Shakespeare? The Murderer, The Motive, The Means.*

'The preacher must have arrived mob-handed. The Corporation appears powerless to stop him. Gastrell was marched out of Stratford "amidst the rages and curses of the inhabitants", and the Corporation passed a by-law forbidding anyone named Gastrell from living in the town.'

Good riddance to bad rubbish, but sadly there was little left of New Place, and an architectural national treasure was lost forever. Twenty-first-century excavation works on the site of *chez* Will have since turned up bits of broken pottery, clay pipes and even an old penny, but at the time of going to press, the search for the holy grail of one of the Bard's old quills or even, perhaps, a wooden trunk brimming with original manuscripts, has proved elusive in the wreckage wrought by the deplorable Reverend Francis Gastrell.

THE FOLIO'S FRENCH CONNECTION

1762

It was but a few, brief pages ago that we delved into the story behind the publication of the First Folio of Shakespeare's collected works in 1623. We learned, in jingoistic horror, that the first print run of the Folio was only made possible by paper imported from our Gallic cousins from across the Channel and this unusual tale is another based on the fabled Folio and an unlikely French connection.

The story begins in 1593 when Jesuit priest, Robert Parsons, headed to the northern French coast and founded a college at Saint-Omer. A Catholic education was forbidden in Blighty at the time and Parsons was forced into his foreign foray to avoid such religious bigotry. The enticement of Duty Free was merely an added bonus.

The next 169 years proved blissfully uneventful, but in 1762 Parsons' school was abruptly expelled from France, and after brief sojourns in Belgium, first in Bruges and then Liège, the school headed to England, now much more *laissez faire* about the whole Catholic thing, relocated to Lancashire and renamed itself Stonyhurst College.

Nothing remarkable there, but in its haste to get out of France the college left a few odds and sods behind, and the public library in Saint-Omer 'inherited' them. In 2014 the library was preparing an exhibition on English literature and, as members of staff searched the shelves for interesting items, they only ruddy found a First Folio.

Experts were despatched to confirm the veracity of the discovery and after lots of beard stroking and magnifying glass wafting, it was confirmed a rare copy of a first edition Folio had indeed been unearthed. *Sacre bleu*!

'First Folios don't turn up very often,' enthused Professor Eric Rasmussen, the man sent to France to confirm the find. 'And when they do, it's usually a really chewed up, uninteresting copy. But this one is magnificent.' He neglected to mention the Folio was missing its title pages and several other introductory pages but it was still jolly exciting.

Now would probably be a good time to put the discovery into some cultural and, yes, financial context. You may remember that experts believe there were only around 800 copies of the first edition Folio printed. The Saint-Omer copy was only the 233rd ever to be found, making it rarer than an Anglophile in the Napoleonic Army.

In terms of cold, hard cash, it is certainly worth a few bob. In 2001 Paul Allen, the co-founder of Microsoft no less, stumped up $6.1 million for his copy of a First Folio, while five years later another first edition went for £2.5 million, when it was auctioned at Sotheby's in London.

So Stonyhurst had simply left behind a hugely valuable First Folio in France. Careless to say the least, but the blow of learning that the college had made such a costly error was significantly softened by the knowledge that the school already owned another precious first edition of the Folio, bequeathed to it by former pupil Lord Arundell. And you need to have a very special library card indeed to take that copy home to help with your GCSE English coursework.

THE FEMININE PRINCE

1776

When Shakespeare was in his pomp, 'women in the theatre' merely meant the fairer sex, preferably seated demurely in the audience, watching his plays. Ladies were not permitted to act professionally in the early seventeenth century for fear of a complete breakdown of polite society and, who knows, it might have put ideas in their silly little heads.

This patriarchal edict precipitated the bizarre tradition of young fellas playing the female roles on stage. Like a six-foot-six drag queen with hands like shovels and an Adam's apple the size of Ayers Rock, they weren't really fooling anyone, but the law was the law and propriety had to be preserved.

However, the Restoration of the monarchy and the coronation of Charles II in 1660 changed all that. Charlie was a keen theatregoer but he was right royally miffed one night when a play he was watching was delayed because one of the actors playing a female role failed to appear on stage on time. The thespian in question was still frantically shaving to prepare for the part and the King issued an edict in 1662 that all female roles should be filled by women.

The dramatic floodgates were open. Actresses streamed onto the stage in ever-increasing numbers, and suddenly, Shakespeare's iconic female characters like Juliet, Lady Macbeth, Desdemona and Miranda had a new-found ring of authenticity.

The ladies continued to tread the boards for the next century but there was still one last theatrical frontier to be explored. If the men could play female roles, why couldn't the women take on male parts? A hearty dose of smelling salts was required to revive the more conservative elements in literary circles when they heard the idea, but the time had finally come for genuine gender equality on stage.

One of the trailblazers for the female members of Equity was Sarah Siddons, who holds the considerable distinction of being the first woman on record to play Hamlet. In terms of plum roles, the Prince of Denmark was undoubtedly the Everest of theatre land, and over a 30-year period Siddons played the tortured Dane nine times.

'In 1775 the young Sarah Siddons – whose father had been trained by Fanny Furnival and was even rumoured to have married her – was spotted in Worcester by the Rev. Henry Bate,' explained Tony Howard in his book *Women as Hamlet: Performance and Interpretation in Theatre, Film and Fiction.* 'He wrote to David Garrick [remember him?] that "the woman Siddons" was a startling talent with a "good breeches figure" and amazing cultural pretensions.'

With her reputation growing, Siddons decided to take the big gamble and, in 1776, she took to the stage in Birmingham and then Manchester as the Bard's titular character. She reprised the role in Liverpool two years later while audiences in Bristol, Edinburgh and Dublin were also witness to her turn as the famed Prince. Her performance in Ireland garnered particular praise for the quality of the fight scenes, the result of Siddons' meticulous preparation and hours of practice with noted swordsman Galindo.

Unsurprisingly others were quick to don their tights and prosthetic codpieces. Her friend Elizabeth Inchbald had a stab at the Dane in 1780 and a succession of aspiring actresses also played Hamlet in the years that followed. 'Neither she [Inchbald] nor Siddons risked the part publicly in London but in 1785 the royal family did Siddons "the honour to hear her read her part of *Hamlet*,"' wrote Howard. 'Other actresses began to emulate her, including Mrs Balkley in Edinburgh that year and Mrs Edmead in York (1792). In 1796 at Drury Lane, Jane Powell became probably the first actress to play Hamlet in London, presented by Siddons' younger brother.'

Thanks to Siddons, one of the last theatrical taboos was broken and nothing was off limits to the girls. It did rather complicate the dressing room arrangements and predictably there were the heated discussions whether the Prince of Denmark's famous line, 'Frailty, thy name is woman!' really added anything to the narrative, but the idea that Hamlet wasn't exclusively a job for the boys had taken root.

THE LOVE THAT DARE NOT WRITE ITS NAME?

1780

Was Shakespeare gay? Or perhaps bisexual? It's a debate that has raged in academia at least since the late eighteenth century and although in our mercifully more enlightened times the answer is neither here nor there, it's a discussion which has engaged some of the finest scholarly minds. And one or two more prurient ones.

The brouhaha about the Bard's sexuality all kicked off in 1780 when a chap called Edmund Malone published a reprint of a collection of Will's poems and sonnets. Nothing particularly remarkable in that, but Malone made the pivotal decision to print the original versions, which meant all the pronouns reverted back to their masculine rather than feminine form.

It was back in 1640 that one John Benson had published an earlier collection of the sonnets, and in some kind of Puritan haze changed all the 'hes' and 'hims' to 'shes' and 'hers', because he was concerned that some of the dedications in his odes made by Will looked a little, well, gay. The arrival of Malone's edition seemed to strip away the polite veneer of heterosexuality and suddenly the academics were asking whether in fact the Bard had written his sonnets and poems to a male lover.

With Malone's new edition on the shelves, it became evident Will had addressed 126 sonnets to someone described both as 'Fair Lord' and 'Fair Youth'. His poems were dedicated to an enigmatic 'Mr W.H.' and with frequent reference to the phrase 'master-mistress of my passion' in Sonnet 20, it did not take long for more censorious scholars to put two and two together, come up with five and jump to the conclusion that Shakespeare was a friend of Dorothy.

'It is impossible to read this fulsome panegyrick,' wrote the noted Shakespearean editor George Steevens in 1780, 'addressed to a male object, without an equal mixture of disgust and indignation.' An alternative camp could not countenance the thought of Will lusting after men, Samuel Taylor Coleridge insisting if the sonnets were indeed written to a fella then the Bard's love was 'pure' and 'chaste' (admiration from a distance, if you will), while others are adamant he was an active homosexual and the pointless row has rumbled on ever since.

Shakespeare's sexuality is not the interesting part here though, it is the identity of the mysterious 'Mr W.H.' and the quest to discover his identity. The search is already more than 200 years old but W.H. has proved more elusive than the von Trapps playing hide-and-seek.

A leading candidate is a piece of eye candy called Henry Wriothesley, aka the third Earl of Southampton, to whom the Bard dedicated his poems *Venus and Adonis* and *The Rape of Lucrece*. Henners was by all accounts a good-looking chap and not averse to 'hug in his arms and play wantonly with' other chaps. His initials were obviously H.W. and not W.H. but the transposition could simply have been Shakespeare adding a little mystery to his dedication.

Other possible Shakespearean paramours include William Haughton, a contemporary dramatist, and Willie Hughes, a dashing young actor who we're not sure even existed. Other theories have it W.H. was an early seventeenth-century William Hall who worked on some of the Bard's texts, while others maintain there never was a male lover and W.H. was simply a spelling mistake and it was the Bard's initials, 'W.S.', which should have appeared.

We'll probably never know – or particularly care – what Will got up to in the privacy of his own bedroom or, for that matter, somebody else's. The salient point here is if you are going to write illicit love poetry don't identify, however obliquely, the object of your desires.

CATHERINE'S THEATRICAL TRANSLATION

1786

It was that pugnacious little chap Napoleon Bonaparte who famously remarked that 'history is a set of lies that people have agreed upon.' Boney wasn't wrong, the past is littered with individuals who are erroneously remembered for things that never happened and, like coffee stain on a fresh white shirt, a besmirched reputation is a bugger to clean.

The Emperor Nero, for example, certainly didn't fiddle with his harpsichord while Rome burned; Lady Godiva didn't ride *au naturel* through the streets of eleventh-century Coventry; and Marie-Antoinette never advocated a gateau-only diet for the denizens of Paris.

Another victim of outrageous historical misreporting is Catherine the Great, the longest-serving female ruler of Russia and a woman who presided over huge territorial gains for her country, and was responsible for initiating an unprecedented building programme and far-reaching economic and political reforms. And yet what do many remember her for? The apocryphal story that she died while engaged in an amorous assignation with a horse.

No, Catherine was definitely Great and if you were to require further evidence of Cathy's credentials, look no further than her self-proclaimed admiration for the Bard. The Empress was in fact such a big fan that she even penned her own dramatic tributes to Stratford's favourite son.

She was a prolific writer, producing 14 comedies, nine opera texts and seven proverbs (short plays) during her lifetime, and, in 1786, she decided it was time to put down her admiration for Shakespeare in black and white. Catherine had also recently had Peter the Great's Winter Palace on the banks of the River Neva demolished and replaced with her shiny new Hermitage Theatre and she was on the lookout for new dramas to grace the venue.

She first turned to *The Merry Wives of Windsor* for inspiration. What she produced was a translation-cum-adaptation, or as she herself described it, an 'imitation' of the Bard's original work, called *What it is to Have Linen and Buck-baskets*, the first ever Russian play to credit Shakespeare's influence. She repeated the trick when she wrote *The Spendthrift*, based on *Timon of Athens*.

Both of the Empresses' babies were performed at the Hermitage and received with rapturous applause. Which had absolutely nothing whatsoever to do with the imminent threat of execution had any member of the audience been deemed not to have appreciated her dramatic efforts.

Catherine is not the only world leader to have had a stab at adapting the Bard. The last King of Poland, Stanislaus August Poniatowski, translated *Julius Caesar* into French (the language of the Polish royal court) in the eighteenth century while Julius Nyerere, the first president of Tanzania, ensured twentieth-century Swahili speakers could enjoy Shakespeare's Roman tragedy and *The Merchant of Venice* in their native tongue.

Queen Victoria reputedly once started an adaptation of *The Comedy of Errors* but abandoned the project when she realised she was not in the least bit amused.

PRESIDENTIAL VANDALISM

1786

Depending on who you choose to believe, it was either Oscar Wilde or George Bernard Shaw who observed that England and America were 'two countries separated by a common language'. We can leave the two literary heavyweights to posthumously argue that one out because our focus here is the Bard and our American cousins across the pond.

Despite the alleged linguistic barrier, Shakespeare has always been a big hit in the United States. Not so much perhaps with bemused High School students, tortured by his impenetrable turn of phrase or references to 'milk maids' or the 'beast with two backs', but overall we can say Will cracked the USA.

He's certainly had more than a few admirers in the White House. Abraham Lincoln once recited the opening soliloquy from *Richard II* to stave off boredom while sitting for a portrait. Ronald Reagan could reel off the 'To-morrow, and to-morrow, and to-morrow' speech from *Macbeth* from memory, while Bill Clinton could do the same, claiming the dialogue reminded him of 'the dangers of blind ambition, the fleeting nature of fame, the ultimate emptiness of power disconnected from higher purpose.' If only the Bard had penned something about the folly of gettin' jiggy with the interns.

Before that trio of Presidential Stratfordians, however, there were John Adams and Thomas Jefferson, the second and third Commander-in-Chiefs respectively, and two men who seriously admired our Will.

'Let me search for the clue which led great Shakespeare into the labyrinth of human nature,' Adams once wrote. 'Let me examine how men think.' Jefferson was equally besotted, insisting, 'Shakespeare must be singled out by one who wishes to learn the full powers of the English language.'

The pair were firm friends and after the conclusion of the American War of Independence (USA 1, Blighty 0), Adams was despatched to England in 1785 by the new government as the first ambassador to Britain. The following year Jefferson took to the boat to join him for a bit of a catch-up and the duo decided to take a little pilgrimage to Stratford-upon-Avon. After all, they could claim it back on expenses.

They duly visited the house on Henley Street where Will was born but the experience proved something of a disappointment. Adams observed in his diary that the house was 'as small and mean as you can conceive. There is nothing preserved of this great genius ... which might inform us what education, what company, what accident turned his mind to letters and drama.'

The gift shop must have had a run on audio guides that particular day, but the two future Presidents were determined to make the most of their trip, despite Jefferson's repeated complaints about the cost of Shakespeare-themed tea cloths and novelty Bard pencil sharpeners, and decided to help themselves to a souvenir of their own. More precisely, they hacked off a chunk of the chair where our Will was reputed to have sat, more than 150 years earlier.

It was a disgraceful act of cultural vandalism, which Adams nonetheless attempted to justify, claiming it was merely 'according to the custom', but since the security guard was evidently enjoying his elevenses at the time, their crime went unpunished.

Jefferson however was not convinced their illicit memento

was the real deal, reasoning that if everyone who visited the house whittled off a bit of wood, there'd be no bloody chair left. 'A chip cut from an armed chair in the chimney corner in Shakespeare's house at Stratford on Avon,' he noted, 'said to be the identical chair in which he usually sat. If true, like the relics of the saints, it must miraculously reproduce itself.' The pilfering pair took their clandestine prize back to the States regardless.

Thousands of American tourists follow in Adams' and Jefferson's footsteps today, flocking to Stratford-upon-Avon every year to sample the atmosphere of the Bard's birthplace. All are thoroughly searched for Swiss Army penknives and nail files before they're allowed near any of the town's historic sites.

WILL'S STELLAR
RECOGNITION

1787

Let's talk about Uranus. Stop giggling at the back, this concerns the English language's greatest-ever writer and you're just lowering the tone now. Right, where were we? Uranus, the seventh planet in the Solar System and the third largest. Discovered by Sir William Herschel in 1781 and, unfortunately, named Ouranos after the Latinised version of the Greek god of the sky.

It is though the 27 moons that orbit Uranus that bring us seamlessly back to the Bard. The first two of the 27 satellites were spotted by Herschel through his prolific telescope six years after his original discovery and everyone in astronomical circles was jolly impressed but in all the excitement nobody bothered to give either moon a name.

The job fell to Herschel's son John a full 71 years later. The tradition was to name new celestial bodies after figures from Greek mythology but John was something of an original thinker and opted to plough his own furrow. Ouranos, he mused, was the god of the sky and logically he'd be surrounded by ethereal spirits, wouldn't he? So how's about calling his dad's moons after two of literature's most famous aerial characters? And so it came to pass that Herschel's satellites were christened Oberon, the King of the Fairies in *A Midsummer Night's Dream*, and Titania, his wife and Queen.

Herschel Junior's bold decision in 1852 set the precedent

and since then all Uranus' moons have taken inspiration from literature. Three of the satellites – Ariel, Umbriel and Belinda – owe their names to characters from Alexander Pope's poem *The Rape of the Lock*, but the rest are strictly Shakespearean in inspiration, and it is now official policy of the catchily titled Working Group for Planetary System Nomenclature to turn to the Bard whenever a new satellite of Uranus is identified.

Recent discoveries include the two small inner moons, which were spotted by the Hubble Space Telescope in 2003 and dubbed Cupid (*Timon of Athens*) and Mab (*Romeo and Juliet*), while the latest addition to the family came in 2015 and was named Margaret after Hero's servant in *Much Ado About Nothing*.

The Shakespeare connection to the Solar System goes further still and out there somewhere are various asteroids called 171 Ophelia, 666 Desdemona and 2758 Cordelia, among others, whizzing around in the vacuum of space.

Ironically Will himself was not apparently a great admirer of the moon. 'O, swear not by the moon,' Juliet says, 'the fickle moon, th' inconstant moon, that monthly changes in her circle orb, Lest that thy love prove likewise variable.'

LEAR'S DRAMATIC SUSPENSION

1788

For a playwright revered around the world, Shakespeare has posthumously endured some pretty shoddy treatment at the hands of censorious authorities. The Bard boasts a global legion of fans but he has not always proved everyone's cup of char.

In 1934, for example, the French government banned performances of *Coriolanus* because the play was deemed unpatriotic. The outbreak of the Second World War precipitated a brief outlawing of his works in Germany, while Israel took *Hamlet* off the menu in 1989 at detention camps for Palestinians, lest the Prince of Denmark's soliloquy about taking up arms 'against a Sea of troubles' should give anyone mischievous ideas. Schools in New Hampshire, USA, banned *Twelfth Night* in 1996 because there was a prohibition on both 'alternative lifestyle instruction' and, it appears, a decent, rounded education.

One of the earliest incidents of Will falling foul of fragile sensibilities was closer to home and began in the late eighteenth century when England was wrestling with the embarrassing problem of an unhinged Royal. Please feel free to insert your own Prince Philip jokes here but we are talking about George III and his long battle with mental illness. The King was not well and everybody knew it.

The problem for those in contemporary theatre land carrying the Shakespearean torch was that the plot of *King*

Lear and its depiction of a tortured monarch descending into insanity was rather too prescient and uncomfortably close to the bone given the current circumstances. Something had to give and in 1788 the managers of the theatres at Drury Lane and Covent Garden both agreed to shelve future productions of the play.

It was a form of voluntary censorship, but the ban was piecemeal and when, in 1810, George's condition worsened dramatically, the authorities implemented a blanket ban on the staging of *Lear* at any theatre in the country.

'In the midst of changes to the discourse in both theatre and medicine, there was, unavoidably, the King,' explained *The Encyclopedia of Romantic Literature*. 'King George III's condition was discussed in Parliament and in the newspapers. This period saw a marked rise in pamphlets debating diagnosis and treatment of madness, with reference to the King's physicians. More abstractly, the 1810 ban on performances of *King Lear* in London theatres acknowledged the connection between Lear and George III. Despite some evidence suggesting that the King's doctors suggested his ailment was "delirium" stemming from fever, rather than the more stigmatised diagnosis "madness", most people associated the King's condition with madness. While direct comparisons with King George III and Lear would seem taboo even before the 1810 ban ... the market was ripe for texts exploring issues of madness.'

The nationwide moratorium on *Lear* would last for ten years and was only lifted months after George's death but the twist in the tale is provided by the theatrical tradition of burlesque which, in this context, has absolutely nothing to do with shapely ladies in lacy undergarments but rather the parodying of a famous dramatic work for comic effect.

'As with most Shakespeare plays, *King Lear* was a popular subject of burlesque,' wrote Dr Lynne Bradley in *Adapting King Lear for the Stage*. '[There were] two Lear burlesques performed early on: *King Lear and his Three Daughters*, performed at the Royalty Theatre in 1812, and *The Lear of Private Life! Or, Father and Daughter*, performed at the Coburg in 1820. These burlesques avoided the performance ban placed on *King Lear*.'

Plans for *King Lear: An Extravaganza on Ice* sadly never came to fruition, principally because it was a terrible idea.

IRELAND'S DOCUMENTARY FAUX PAS

1796

'The first lesson of economics is scarcity,' observed the American social commentator Thomas Sowell. 'There is never enough of anything to fully satisfy all those who want it.' Clever chap, Thomas, and when you consider the supply and demand dynamics of commodities, such as Cabbage Patch Kid dolls circa 1983, Glastonbury tickets, or honest Members of Parliament, his assertion definitely holds water.

In late eighteenth-century England it was no different and the great, unsatiated public appetite was for biographical information about Shakespeare. The Bard's fame was growing and as his posthumous popularity increased, the hunger for insights into his life rose. In short, there was a gaping gap in the market.

Step forward author and engraver Samuel Ireland who announced in 1796 with much trumpet and fanfare that his son, William Henry, had unearthed the mother lode of all things Shakespearean, including two previously unknown plays, as well as assorted letters, documents and stuff like that. The Irelands duly published *Miscellaneous Papers and Legal Instruments under the Hand and Seal of William Shakespeare*, and a copy of *Vortigern and Rowena*, the lost tragedy they claimed had been penned by the Bard himself.

Their find was nothing short of a sensation as the public voraciously pored over the documentary titbits but as you've probably already deduced, there was something decidedly fishy about the *Miscellaneous Papers*, which mobilised the sceptics who suspected the Irelands were trying to pull a fast one.

Chief among the doubters was Edmond Malone, the leading Shakespearean scholar of the era, who smelled a large rodent right from the start and quickly published a forensic, 400-page dissection of the book entitled, *An Inquiry Into the Authenticity of Certain Miscellaneous Papers and Legal Instruments.* In it Malone painstakingly pointed out the myriad of linguistic incongruities and historical mistakes, as well as examples of faked handwriting samples and other errors, and concluded the Irelands had produced nothing more than a poorly-executed fraud.

Worse followed for the duplicitous father-and-son team when *Vortigern and Rowena* received its première in London. It was a sell-out, but anticipation quickly turned to near anarchy as the audience failed to be captivated by the drama on offer, and the production had to be temporarily halted as order was restored. It was the play's first and only performance. Ireland Junior blamed the actors, and alleged a mob of Malone devotees had infiltrated the theatre, but the truth was that *Vortigern and Rowena* sucked.

Samuel Ireland refused to acknowledge *Miscellaneous Papers* wasn't worth the paper it was written on and published a book designed to destroy Malone's academic credibility. The main thrust of his argument was that Malone relied too heavily on handwriting analysis and silly things like facts in his rebuttal, and that it was all a matter of literary taste and interpretation, but nobody was listening. Especially when, in 1805, his son broke ranks and wrote *The Confessions of William Henry Ireland* in which he admitted in black and white that he had indeed made it all up.

Ireland Junior insisted his father had played no part in the deception but by this stage nobody believed anything they said. 'The hopeful youth takes on himself the guilt of the entire forgery, and strains hard to exculpate his worthy father from the slightest participation in it', the scholar George Steevens had written in 1796. 'The father, on the contrary, declares that his son had not sufficient abilities for the execution of so difficult a task. Between them, in short, there is a pretended quarrel, that they may not look as if they were acting in concert on the present occasion.'

The upshot of the whole sorry affair was the ruination of both Samuel and William's reputations, which was probably no less than they deserved, but their fate evidently did not deter one John Payne Collier from trying to pull off the same fraudulent trick in 1852, when he went to press with his book *Notes and Emendations to the Text of Shakespeare*.

Essentially a rework of a copy of the Second Folio, the work featured new amendments and corrections to the Bard's plays, which Collier claimed he had uncovered in his new manuscript. The literary establishment took a deep collective breath and promptly demolished Collier, exposing *Notes and Emendations* as a shameless fake.

Literary forgeries of course do not always make it into print and it's a little-known fact that back in 1983 *The Sunday Times* refused to publish extracts from an allegedly autobiographical manuscript entitled *Shakespeare, My Life as a Hawaiian Hula Dancer* and opted instead to print a serialisation of *The Hitler Diaries*.

KEEPING IT IN THE FAMILY

1807

Censorship is a generally a very bad thing. There are times when common sense and decency must prevail – nobody wants the kids picking up their copy of *The Beano* to be confronted with Dennis the Menace f-bombing Granny – but such unlikely expletive-laden scenarios aside, freedom of expression is what we all want.

You would be forgiven for thinking no one would make so bold or be so presumptuous as to censor the Bard's plays but you would clearly be unaware of one Henrietta Bowdler and her quest to make Stratford's finest more acceptable to the younger reader.

Henrietta was a conservative soul. As a young lady she would shut her eyes at the opera throughout a performance because she considered the dancers on stage to be 'indelicate' and her idea of a girls' big night out was probably a cup of warm water at her Aunt Vera's. In short she was pathologically straight-laced but she was well read and she had a problem with our Will.

Her issue was his perceived vulgar tendencies and propensity to bawdy humour, which Henrietta deemed wholly inappropriate for family consumption. The Bard, she decided, needed cleaning up and she set about editing and revising his canon to make it nice and wholesome. The result was the *Family Shakespeare*, published in 1807, a four-volume work featuring 20 plays in their new sanitised form and missing around 10 per cent of the original text, which she dismissed as too rude or raunchy.

'It will, I believe, be universally acknowledged that few authors are so instructive as Shakespeare,' Henrietta wrote in the preface to her magnum opus. 'But his warmest admirers must confess, that his Plays contain much that is vulgar, and much that is indelicate.'

The changes she made were manifest. In *Hamlet*, for example, Ophelia simply drowns rather than committing suicide as is implied in the Bard's original, while Lady Macbeth's famous cry, 'Out, damned spot!' became 'Out, crimson spot!' The prostitute, Doll Tearsheet, in *Henry IV, Part II* was unsurprisingly consigned to the cutting room floor.

The public, however, initially failed to get on board with our self-appointed moral crusader and the *Family Shakespeare* was a flop, but the Bowdler family was nothing if not puritanically persistent and in 1818 Henrietta's brother, Dr Thomas, had another stab at it, publishing a new ten-volume edition of all of Will's plays with all the naughty bits expunged.

The second book met with a more favourable reaction from those terrified the Bard was corrupting the youth of the age, but history has been less kind to the brother and sister duo, with the expression to 'bowdlerise' now a pejorative term for editing and censoring original text.

More recent attempts to 'bowdlerise' literary titles have proved unsuccessful with the two-page, 500-word version of *Fifty Shades of Grey* in particular failing to fly off the shelves.

TOP MARX
FOR THE BARD
1844

Money is a serious business. Benny and Björn may been laughing all the way to the bank after Abba sang 'Money, money, money, must be funny, in a rich man's world' in 1976 to record yet another chart topper, but on the whole there's very little comical about matters monetary.

Karl Marx certainly didn't crack a smile when he turned his famed mind to financial issues. The German philosopher described money as the 'common whore' in his pamphlet *Economic and Philosophic Manuscripts of 1844*, and berated financial fetishism, the alienation of man by a lack of spending power and how society was perverted by the perpetual pursuit of more wealth. Barclays cancelled his current account when they read all that.

The Shakespearean element to this discourse can be found later in *Economic and Philosophic Manuscripts* when Marx directly quoted the Bard to expand on his argument that money was amoral and corrosive. He chose *Timon of Athens* and a speech from the titular character in Act IV, Scene III of the play to make his point:

Gold? Yellow, glittering, precious gold?
No, Gods, I am no idle votarist! …
Thus much of this will make black white, foul fair,
Wrong right, base noble, old young, coward valiant.
… Why, this

Will lug your priests and servants from your sides,
Pluck stout men's pillows from below their heads:
This yellow slave
Will knit and break religions, bless the accursed;
Make the hoar leprosy adored, place thieves
And give them title, knee and approbation
With senators on the bench:
This is it That makes the wappen'd widow wed again;
She, whom the spital-house and ulcerous sores
Would cast the gorge at, this embalms and spices
To the April day again. Come, damned earth,
Thou common whore of mankind, that put'st odds
Among the rout of nations.

'Shakespeare stresses especially two properties of money,'
Marx observed of Timon's words. 'It is the visible divinity –
the transformation of all human and natural properties into
their contraries, the universal confounding and distorting of
things: impossibilities are soldered together by it. It is the
common whore, the common procurer of people and nations.'

Whether the Bard would have approved of being
appropriated in this way by the co-author of *The Communist
Manifesto* is debatable, but since he was six feet under
he couldn't really object, and Marx was able to gild his
economic treatise without protest.

Marx was just 26 when he wrote *Economic and Philosophic
Manuscripts of 1844*. They were not published until 1927
after he had joined Will in the choir invisible and he was
buried in Highgate Cemetery in north London. His
gravestone bears the epitaph 'Workers of All Lands Unite',
but what many admirers don't realise is that while Karl may
have insisted money was the root of all evil, his co-author
Friedrich Engels was not short of a bob or two, and on his
death left Marx's surviving daughters a share of his $4.8
million estate.

DICKENS AND THE SHOWMAN

1847

Most Americans just cannot get enough of British architecture and history. They may not be as enamoured by our dental hygiene, portion sizes or aversion to firearms, but when it comes to old buildings, our cousin from across the pond is spellbound. Show a Yank Windsor Castle or Balmoral for the first time and it's prudent to have a defibrillator on standby.

The American preoccupation with Blighty's architecture was famously in evidence in the 1960s, when the City of London flogged London Bridge to a Missouri millionaire, who then dismantled it, shipped the stone Stateside and rebuilt the bridge in Arizona, but this tale focuses on a smaller, more modest construction.

We are talking about the house on Henley Street in Stratford-upon-Avon in which Will was born. If you can remember as far back as Shakespeare's will (see 'The Great Bed Debate, 1616'), you will recall that the Bard left the house to his eldest daughter Susanna and until the early nineteenth century, the iconic property remained in the family. In 1847, however, the last private owner of the house, a butcher's widow by the name of Mrs Court, popped her clogs and the Bard's gaff was put on the market.

At the same time as the 'For Sale' sign was being erected on Henley Street, the famous American showman and circus owner, P.T. Barnum, just happened to be in England, touring with his latest attraction, Tom Thumb, and when he heard Shakespeare's old home was up for grabs, he quickly sent a representative to try and conclude a deal.

'Americans appreciate the immortal Bard of Avon as keenly as do their brethren in the Mother Country (a Mother of whom we are all justly proud) and I greatly desired to honour the New World by erecting this invaluable relic in its commercial metropolis,' wrote Barnum in his memoirs years later.

'I soon despatched a trusty agent to Stratford-upon-Avon, armed with the cash and full powers to buy the Shakespeare House and have it carefully taken down, packed in boxes and shipped to New York. He was cautioned not to whisper my name and to give no hint that the building was ever to leave England.'

Barnum's 'man' must have whispered something to somebody though because news that the brash American was planning to take such a great cultural treasure out of the country did leak out. Something had to be done and in time-honoured British tradition a committee was formed. Among its number was none other than literary heavyweight, Charles Dickens, who had no intention of allowing Henley Street to be appropriated by Barnum. The group quickly raised £3,000, outbid our American circus master at auction and the historic house was saved.

'Some English gentlemen got wind of the transaction and bought the house,' wrote Barnum. 'I fancy there would have been an excitement and use of printer's ink equalling that caused by my purchasing the great African elephant Jumbo from the London Zoo 38 years later.'

Dickens and Co. – the 'English gentlemen' – had dubbed themselves the 'Shakespeare Birthday Committee', but a private Act of Parliament saw the group renamed the 'Shakespeare Birthday Trust', and it is this organisation that today looks after the five heritage sites in Stratford connected to the Bard.

Barnum headed back to the States after being outmanoeuvred by Blighty's finest, but subsequently claimed that had he and Shakespeare been contemporaries, he could have made him famous by putting him on stage. We'll never know whether he was being ironic or not.

THE GREAT AUTHORSHIP DEBATE

1848

The power of the imagination is a wonderful thing. Without regular flights of imaginative fancy the world would be bereft of some of the greatest works of art and literature while playtime at primary school without a dash of childish invention would become very prosaic indeed.

Shakespeare's imagination was formidable but for some sceptics in the mid-nineteenth century, the Bard was perhaps a little too imaginative for his own good. This, dear reader, marks the beginning of the great authorship debate and the ongoing question of who truly penned the Shakespearean canon. It's a long dialogue so you might want to pop the kettle on before we start.

The basic tenet of the argument that Will did not write the plays that bear his name in black and white is that he was far too provincial and relatively uneducated to have pulled it all off. 'His' plays demonstrated intimate knowledge of exotic foreign lands, politics, royal courts and aristocratic affairs, yet Shakespeare was no more than a parochial bumpkin from Warwickshire, who had never been to university and, as far as we can prove, never even travelled abroad.

Defenders of our Will have always countered this argument with one simple response. He. Used. His. Imagination. After all, Jules Verne didn't tunnel extensively before writing *Journey to the Centre of the Earth,* Ray Bradbury had never been to Mars before penning *The Martian Chronicles* and

J.K. Rowling presumably had never made the acquaintance of a single witch or wizard before starting work on the *Harry Potter* series. They used their imagination.

The Anti-Stratfordians, as the doubters are dubbed, also point out Will came from an illiterate family and argue his range of literary style is too well executed to have come from the humble quill of a man with such a modest background.

The whole Anti-Stratfordian movement effectively began in 1848 when a chap called Joseph C. Hart published a book called *The Romance of Yachting* which, despite its misleading title, was the first time anyone had questioned in print whether the Bard really was responsible for the works attributed to him. In 1852 Dr Robert W. Jameson published an article entitled 'Who Wrote Shakespeare?' in the *Edinburgh Journal*, which did exactly what it said on the tin, while four years later the American writer Delia Bacon penned a piece – 'William Shakespeare and His Plays: An Enquiry Concerning Them' – which appeared in *Putnam's Magazine*.

The knives were now well and truly out for poor old Will and although there is an army of academics ready to defend his literary honour, the seeds of doubt had been sown. 'These two notions – that the Shakespeare canon represented the highest achievement of human culture, while William Shakespeare was a completely uneducated rustic,' wrote Michael Dobson in *The Oxford Companion to Shakespeare*, 'combined to persuade Delia Bacon and her successors that the Folio's title page and preliminaries could only be part of a fabulously elaborate charade orchestrated by some more elevated personage, and they accordingly misread the distinctive literary traces of Shakespeare's solid Elizabethan grammar-school education visible throughout the volume as evidence that the "real" author had attended Oxford or Cambridge.'

And so to this 'elevated personage', because the burning question now is, if the Bard didn't write 37 or perhaps even more breathtakingly good dramatic masterpieces, who the hell did? It certainly wasn't Colonel Mustard in the study with the lead piping.

The Anti-Stratfordian lobby becomes a touch fragmented when it comes to supplying an answer to that one and at the last count more than 80 historical figures had been variously put forward as the 'real' Shakespeare. There are also over 5,000 books exploring the whole authorship debate, suggesting a certain lack of consensus.

Like a modern Curly Wurly, life's too short to delve into all the candidates and their claims to be the greatest writer in the history of the English language. At best all are spurious and there is not a single scrap of conclusive documentary evidence to prove any of them were the real power behind the literary throne.

Suffice it to say that in the nineteenth century most Anti-Stratfordians were absolutely convinced Sir Francis Bacon was the man responsible for the plays and used Shakespeare as a front because it would not have been proper for a man of high office – he served as both Attorney General and Lord Chancellor of England – to write for the public stage. More recently Edward de Vere, seventeenth Earl of Oxford, has become jolly popular with those adamant Will couldn't possibly have written the plays. All the theories are based on no more than opinion, interpretation and pure guesswork.

The row between the Stratfordians and Anti-Stratfordians has been rumbling on for decades and took an acrimonious turn in 2011 with the release of the film *Anonymous*, a fictionalised account of de Vere's life, which ran with the inflammatory tagline 'Was Shakespeare a Fraud?'

Despite all the conspiracy theories, however, the weight of academic opinion remains firmly in Will's camp. The Bard may not have been a well-travelled toff with connections but he knew his way around a five-act drama. And, at the risk of repetition, he used his imagination.

ANARCHY AT THE ASTOR

1849

Theatre land is not exactly renowned for its violent underbelly. It's true some patrons can become somewhat fractious when those sitting next to them noisily attempt to open their packet of Fox's Glacier Mints, and police were once called to the Old Vic when two 50-something ladies had curt words over ownership of an umbrella, but overall the theatre is regarded as a pretty safe place to be.

It was an altogether different story in nineteenth-century America. Social tensions between the predominantly American and immigrant Irish working class and the Anglophile upper class in the States were growing, and the theatre increasingly found itself on the front line of the fallout, as the two disparate groups clashed as their respective curtains came down.

'By the 1830s, separate theatres offered separate kinds of performances for rich and poor but violence continued,' according to *Liberty, Equality, Power: A History of the American People*. 'It culminated in the rivalry between the American actor Edwin Forrest and the English actor William Charles Macready. Macready was a trained Shakespearean actor and his restrained style and attention to the subtleties of the text had won him acclaim both in Britain and the United States. Forrest, on the other hand, played to the cheap seats. With his bombast and histrionics, he transformed Shakespeare's tragedies into melodramas.'

Forrest of course was the hero of the working classes while Macready was favoured by the sophisticates. It should have remained simply a dramatic rivalry, but escalated into something much darker in 1849, when the two actors decided to both take the lead in *Macbeth* on the same night in the same town.

Macready was on stage at the Astor Place Theatre in Manhattan, New York City. Forrest was playing the same role at the nearby Bowery Theatre and during Macready's performance, the Astor was invaded by an angry mob of American and Irish workers, who threw chairs and tried to burn the theatre down. Tragically the National Guard had already been mobilised, because the authorities had anticipated trouble, and they opened fire, killing more than 20 people.

The fatal incident has been cited by some as bloody evidence that the curse associated with *Macbeth* is real. It's true that the competing performances of the play that evening framed the fatal events but the spark for the violence that unfolded was all about class divisions rather than a difference of opinion over theatrical styles.

VERDI'S OPERATIC OPT-OUT

1850

Did you know that there are more than 200 operas based on the works of Shakespeare? That's more musical tributes to the genius of the Bard than plays he originally penned, and while this plethora of operas varies wildly in what they retain and what they reject from Will's writing, they share a common inspiration. And a fair share of larger ladies with booming voices and heaving bosoms.

The great Italian composer Giuseppe Verdi turned to the Bard for the template for three of his acclaimed operas. His *Macbeth* premièred in Florence in 1847, *Otello* was debuted at the Teatro alla Scala in Milan 40 years later, while *Falstaff* (based on the iconic character's exploits in both *Henry IV, Part I* and *The Merry Wives of Windsor* and performed first in 1893) was Verdi's final ever opera.

Yep, Giuseppe certainly appreciated Will's knack with a dramatic narrative and his ability to draw complex characters but his deep admiration for the Bard became profound exasperation when he turned his attention to *King Lear*. Verdi was a musical genius but the play was ultimately to defeat even he.

The Italian was desperate to turn *Lear* into an opera and in 1850 he contacted revered librettist (aka lyric writer), Salvadore Cammarano, to discuss the project. 'Re Lear as a play is so vast and interwoven that it would seem to be impossible to fashion an opera from it,' he wrote to

Cammarano. 'But, examining it closely it seems that the challenges, though large, are not insurmountable. You know that you should not treat this play using forms and methods that are familiar, but rather should treat it in an entirely new manner, one that is vast and shows no regard for customary forms.'

'It seems to me that the principal roles are five: Lear, Cordelia, the Fool, Edmund and Edgar. There will be two smaller roles for women (Lear's older daughters), Regana and Gonerilla (the latter perhaps more prominent) and two smaller roles for basses (as in *Luisa Miller*): Kent and Gloucester. All the rest are smaller roles.'

A solid start there from Verdi but Cammarano inconveniently died in 1852 before he could finish his libretto and Verdi turned to one Antonio Somma to supply the words he needed. The pair had a few artistic disagreements along the way but in 1853 Somma had done the business and his four-act libretto was complete.

All that was now required was the music but Verdi suddenly seemed to lose impetus and *Re Lear* stubbornly remained a work of words and no notes. The great composer could not find it in himself to set the story to music and when, in 1865, he dabbled with taking *Lear* to France, he again lost his nerve. '*Re Lear* is magnificent,' he wrote, 'sublime, pathetic, but it does not have enough scenic splendor for the Paris Opera.'

Exactly why Verdi could not bring his project to a conclusion will probably remain a mystery but we do know in 1896, just five years before his death, he offered the libretto to fellow composer Pietro Mascagni, who understandably enquired why the great Verdi would not write the opera himself. 'The scene in which King Lear finds himself on the heath scared me,' was Giuseppe's reply.

Lear is not the only Shakespeare play to have failed to make it off the musical drawing board. 'It is a lesser-known fact that Mozart contemplated writing a version of *The Tempest*,' wrote Gregory Doran in *The Daily Telegraph*. 'Frederick Delius wanted to write an opera of *As You Like It*. Tchaikovsky rejected the idea of writing an opera of *The Merchant of Venice*, but toyed with the idea of writing one based on *Othello*.'

Sadly one musical reworking of Will's work that did come to fruition was a recording of Sir Ian McKellen's recital of Sonnet 18 ('Shall I compare thee to a summer's day' *et al*) set to rap music. 'Shakespeare is all based on beats, rhythm and rhyme, all things that rappers deal with,' enthused Sir Ian while everyone else held their head in their hands and groaned.

PICTURE IMPERFECT

1856

The year 1856 was an eventful one in British history. It signalled the end of the Crimean War after three years of fisticuffs with the Russians, the inaugural Boat Race between Oxford and Cambridge Universities was staged and the Nobel Prize-winning playwright George Bernard Shaw was born. At roughly the same time, a fella by the name of Isaac Spratt registered the rules of modern croquet, but that doesn't quite have the historical resonance we're looking for here.

Oh yes, 1856 was also the year the famed National Portrait Gallery in London was established, the world's first, well, portrait gallery. That belonged to the nation. It was first housed in a modest building in Westminster and boasted an initial collection of just 57 paintings. The very first portrait acquired for the gallery just happened to be one of Shakespeare, and while it was quite the compliment to our Will to be the first mug hung on the new walls, it does rather raise the whole thorny issue of what exactly the Bard looked like and whether the image we have of him in our modern minds is accurate or not.

That inaugural picture in the National Portrait Gallery is the 'Chandos' portrait. It's the default image of the Bard, the most famous representation of Shakespeare in existence, but there's a teeny-weeny problem. Minuscule really, but probably worth mentioning that we have no proof who painted it, when it was created and no firm evidence that it is in fact Shakespeare rather than, say, a random travelling ruff salesman who just happened to wander into an artist's studio at the right time on the right day.

The Chandos has gained fame and a degree of reflected authenticity principally because it was the image on which the engraving on the cover of the First Folio of 1623 was based but to claim that proves it's Shakespeare is akin to photocopying a tenner and swearing blind it's legal tender. Ben Jonson is said to have authenticated the First Folio image as legit but then he also urged readers to 'looke not on his Picture, but his Booke' so his testimony is far from watertight.

Even the National Portrait Gallery have conceded their prized Chandos might not be the real deal. 'We may never find the clincher piece of evidence, though it may yet turn up,' admitted Dr Tarnya Cooper in 2006 when the gallery staged an exhibition of various Shakespeare pictures. 'It would be lovely to be categorical. It is certainly fairly likely we are looking at the face of Shakespeare, but we'd need a document or a signature to prove it beyond all doubt.'

There are many other well-known pretenders to the throne, claiming to be authentic images of the Bard, but all suffer from a lack of supporting documentation or other inconvenient but unavoidable truths, which undermine their credibility. The truth is we do not have a single painting, sketch or engraving which anyone can categorically prove is a true likeness of Will.

The literary world did though get jolly excited in 2015 when a fellow called Mark Griffiths, a botanical historian, screamed from the rooftops that he had discovered a genuine engraving of Shakespeare from his lifetime in a 400-year-old book entitled *The Herball or Generall Historie of Plantes*. Griffiths claimed that he and Edward Wilson, emeritus fellow of Worcester College, Oxford, had spent five years deciphering hidden clues that led to identifying

Will's pic on the inside cover, and they were convinced it was definitely, absolutely, without a shadow of doubt the great man himself. 'We do not think anyone is going to dispute this at all,' said Wilson.

'I'm deeply unconvinced,' said Professor Michael Dobson, director of the Shakespeare Institute at the University of Birmingham, three milliseconds later. 'One has seen so many claims on Shakespeare based on somebody claiming to crack a code. And nobody else has apparently been able to decipher this for 400 years. And there's no evidence that anybody thought that this was Shakespeare at the time.'

What Will's image was supposedly doing in a sixteenth-century gardener's handbook is a moot point. As far as we know he wasn't a keen horticulturist, but he did write *Richard* III and Troilus and *Cress*ida (so very sorry), so maybe the Bard did have green fingers after all.

DELIA'S GRAVE MISTAKE

1856

'Do you know how they are going to settle the Shakespeare-Bacon dispute?' once asked W.S. Gilbert of Gilbert and Sullivan fame after enduring what was apparently a turgid portrayal of Hamlet by an actor by the name of Herbert Beerbohm Tree. 'They are going to dig up Shakespeare and dig up Bacon; they are going to set their coffins side by side, and they are going to get Tree to recite *Hamlet* to them. And the one who turns in his coffin will be the author of the play.'

Gilbert was joking of course but sometimes there is method in the madness if you're desperate enough to find it and this bizarre tale relates the startling case of the Bard's grave and the night in which Will's final resting place was almost desecrated.

Our protagonist is Delia Bacon, the American writer, whom you will remember was one of the first to publicly question whether Shakespeare really wrote 'his' plays. Although no relation, Delia was convinced Francis Bacon was the true author and she was prepared to go to great lengths to prove it.

In 1856 she was over in Blighty on business and decided it was an opportune time to visit the Holy Trinity Church in Stratford-upon-Avon. In fact, she had convinced herself that Will had been buried with documents which would prove her Bacon theory once and for all, and Delia determined she would spend the night at the church, open Will's coffin and unearth her evidence. Shakespeare's ominous epitaph – 'Blest be the man that spares these stones, *And curst be he that moves my bone'* – really should have been ringing in her ears but Delia was intent on unmasking Will as a fraud.

'I had a dark lantern like Guy Fawkes, and some other articles which might have been considered suspicious if the police had come upon us,' she wrote of her night at Holy Trinity. 'I was alone till ten o'clock … all the long drawn aisle was in utter darkness. I had made a promise to the clerk that I would do not the least thing for which he could be called into question, and though I went far enough to see that examination I had proposed to make, could be made, I did not feel at liberty to make it, for fear I might violate the trust this man had reposed in me.'

In short, she bottled it, and come the next morning the Bard's coffin was untouched. Delia left without her smoking gun but she didn't let that little setback deter her and the following year she published *The Philosophy of the Plays of Shakespeare Unfolded*, a heavyweight attack on Will's reputation as a literary genius. Some scholars were much impressed by her arguments and academic rigour while others quite reasonably pointed out that anyone who spends a night in a graveyard with the intention of disinterring corpses had to be just a bit mental.

ABE'S THEATRICAL ASSASSINATION

1865

> All the world's a stage,
> And all the men and women merely players;
> They have their exits and their entrances,
> And one man in his time plays many parts.

The opening lines of Jaques' speech in Act II, Scene VII of *As You Like It* are some of Shakespeare's most enduring and oft quoted and rather apt when we consider the intriguing role the Bard allegedly played in the assassination of Abraham Lincoln at Ford's Theatre in Washington in 1865.

Obviously our Will didn't shoot Abe himself. Not unless he gunned down the sixteenth President of the United States from beyond the grave and the presumed culprit, the notorious John Wilkes Booth, was merely a patsy. There is though a school of thought that argues Shakespeare did indeed play an unwitting part in one of the most infamous murders in modern political history.

So back to 'one man in his time plays many parts', a line which eerily resonates with the life of Booth, a member of a respected theatrical family and acclaimed stage actor in his own right in the States before he somewhat blotted his copybook by blowing the President's brains out. Booth did however play 'many parts' and his other major role was that of Confederate sympathiser and supporter as the American

Civil War was drawing to its close. As the head of the soon-to-be victorious Union, Lincoln was definitely not on his Christmas card list.

Booth's favourite Shakespearean character was Brutus, the slayer of the man he viewed as the (eponymous) evil tyrant in *Julius Caesar*. In November 1864 he appeared in a production of the play alongside his two brothers in New York and, you can see where we're going with this, some scholars believe he ultimately rather blurred the lines between literary fantasy and reality.

When the army of Robert E. Lee surrendered in April 1865, effectively signalling the Confederate's defeat in the Civil War, Booth could apparently take it no longer, and five days after the humiliation, headed to Washington for his bloody date with destiny.

'As he fled across the boards of Ford's Theatre to the horse that awaited him in the alley, he must have been convinced that he had identified himself forever with the role that Shakespeare had scripted for antiquity's most notable assassin,' wrote the president of the Shakespeare Guild, John F. Andrews, in a 1990 article. 'What Booth may not have realized was that he had cast himself even more indelibly in the role of antiquity's most infamous villain.'

There are a number of fascinating footnotes to what is an already intriguing tale.

Lincoln himself was a lifelong fan of Shakespeare's work and in the days leading up his assassination is said to have read aloud from the speech in *Macbeth* about the death of King Duncan. 'After life's fitful fever,' the title character intones, 'he sleeps well.' Spooky or what?

In Booth's diary, he wrote that he shouted 'Sic semper' as he pulled the trigger. The phrase 'Sic semper tyrannis' ('thus always to tyrants') is frequently attributed to the real Brutus after he stabbed Caesar in 44BC. You can't argue with history, can you?

The proceeds from the Booth brothers' acclaimed

performance of *Julius Caesar* five months before the killing were put towards the erection of a statue of, wait for it, William Shakespeare. It still stands today in Central Park in New York.

William Shakespeare is an anagram of 'I Shot Abraham Lincoln'. OK, it's not really.

However, it is worth pointing out that the play Abe was watching before Booth brutally punched his ticket was a production of *Our American Cousin* by the English wordsmith Tom Taylor, so you can't touch the Bard for that.

Booth's 'stage exit' came 14 days after the assassination when he was cornered by a posse of soldiers in rural Virginia and shot in the neck. Sadly for the symmetry of our tale, he did not have a heavily thumbed copy of *Julius Caesar* on him.

HARRY'S HOTSPURS

1882

Shakespeare was evidently not a fan of Association Football. The Bard mentions the beautiful game just twice in his entire body of work and while he is exceedingly free and easy with his nods to the Bible, the Royal Court or the wonders of the natural world, for example, football is conspicuous by its absence. Especially when we consider 50 other sports are also mentioned.

Dromio of Ephesus fleetingly mentions the sport in Act II, Scene I in *The Comedy of Errors,* but we perhaps get a clearer insight into Will's own views of the game when the Earl of Kent dismisses Oswald as a 'base football player', in Act I, Scene IV of *King Lear*. So probably not a season ticket holder at Aston Villa then.

There's a certain irony in that Shakespeare unwittingly played a hand in the naming of Tottenham Hotspur, the famous London club which, over a century ago, took its name from one of the Bard's most famous characters.

The year was 1882 and a group of local boys from St John's Presbyterian Grammar School decided it was high time they formed a new football club. They all agreed that 'St John's FC' just didn't have the right ring to it, and after discounting the 'Presbyterian Players' as well, they opted for 'Hotspur FC'. That's Hotspur as in Harry Percy, the daring and valiant knight, immortalised by the Bard in *Henry IV, Part I.*

In the interests of full and forthright disclosure, we cannot be absolutely 100 per cent sure our young footballers did turn to Shakespeare for inspiration but it is certainly possible. Hotspur's name was synonymous with his derring-do and his heroics in battle, and it is no coincidence that the club's motto '*Audere est Facere*' translates as 'To Dare is to Do'.

There is also a historical connection between Percy's family and the area of north London where the football club is located, with the Northumberlands reputed to have owned extensive tracts of land surrounding the stadium.

Our footballers were jolly pleased with their new set-up until it was pointed out that there was, in fact, already a team called Hotspur FC in London that had been around for four years and they were not best pleased with the attempt to brazenly appropriate their name. A tweak was required and after briefly toying with the idea of going with Northumberland Hotspur, in 1884 they plumped for Tottenham Hotspur.

But back to the Bard, who may not have been an avid football fan but he was mad for the *American* football, famously throwing the winning touchdown pass for Notre Dame against Ohio State in 1935, a game that was subsequently voted the greatest ever college football match in the States. OK, it was one William Valentine Shakespeare and not *our* Will who threw that pass, but the shared name did provide the sports hacks of the day with the unmissable opportunity to dub the young Valentine variously as 'The Bard of Staten Island', 'The Bard of South Bend' and 'The Merchant of Menace'. They missed a trick though. 'The Taming of the Threw'? No? Suit yourself then.

DEM BONES, DEM BONES

1883

If you've ever watched an episode of *Silent Witness*, *CSI* or even *Diagnosis: Murder* (starring as it did not only Dick van Dyke but, double your money, his son Barry), then you may be familiar with the process of forensic facial reconstruction. Take one skull, recreate the missing muscle and skin and, hey presto, you've got the face of your unidentified murder victim, and you're one step closer to solving the case.

Forensic facial reconstruction has been around longer than you might think and it was as far back as 1883 that a German anatomist named Hermann Welcker was credited with creating the first three-dimensional facial approximation from cranial remains.

It was also in 1883 that a chap called Dr Clement Mansfield Ingleby controversially suggested Shakespeare should be exhumed, his skull taken to the nearest lab, and his face reconstructed. Ingelby made his macabre proposal in a pamphlet, *Shakespeare's Bones*, and he was deadly serious about ignoring the curse the Bard had purportedly penned for his final resting place and relying on science to provide the answer to the big unresolved question of what the Bard *really* looked like.

'Why, I ask, should not an attempt be made to recover Shakespeare's skull?' wrote Ingleby. 'Why should not the authorities of Stratford, to whom this brochure is inscribed, sanction, or even themselves undertake, a respectful examination of the grave in which Shakespeare's remains are believed to have been buried? Beyond question, the skull of Shakespeare, might we but discover it in anything like its condition at the time of its interment, would be of still greater interest and value ... I would forthwith perform the exploration, and if possible obtain tangible proof that the poet's skull had not been removed from its resting-place.'

The 'authorities of Stratford' however refused to play ball, reasoning that if any bit of Will had indeed been 'removed' it might hit the tourist trade and, if his skull was discovered intact, any subsequent facial reconstruction might conflict with the image depicted by the Bard's funerary monument (see 'Immovable in Death, 1616'), which was housed inside Holy Trinity Church. It was, they concluded, a bad idea all around.

Ingleby was gutted but there was no court of appeal and Shakespeare's skeleton remained undisturbed. Three years later the good doctor himself was worm food after succumbing to ill health and no one since has been so indelicate as to suggest the Bard should be dug up.

THE BARD
CAUSES BIRD STRIKE
1890

Shakespeare impacts on different people in different ways. For some he is a lifelong friend and his work an enduring inspiration, while for others the Bard is no more than a passing acquaintance, a section of the GCSE English syllabus to be studied but soon forgotten. Our Will has always elicited a wide range of reactions.

The impression he made on an American by the name of Eugene Schieffelin though was most peculiar indeed and was the catalyst for a bizarre chain of events that would ultimately lead to the untimely death of 62 people in the States.

Schieffelin belonged to the New York Zoological Society, and was also a member of the American Acclimatization Society, a group that aimed to facilitate the exchange of plants and animals from one continent to another in the name of biodiversity. But when Eugene wasn't immersed in the natural world, he was an avid reader of the Bard and, after thumbing his way through the plays and sonnets, he determined to attempt to introduce all of the bird species mentioned by Shakespeare to America, which were not already native to the country.

There are over 600 references to birds in Will's *oeuvre* from swans to doves, robins to starlings and swallows to wrens, but Schieffelin had no joy when he released bullfinches, chaffinches, nightingales and skylarks, which all found conditions across the Atlantic not to their liking and failed to acclimatise or breed.

So which species next? Eugene was nothing if not thorough, and although there is just one solitary reference to starlings in the entire Shakespearean canon – it is uttered by Hotspur in Act I, Scene III of *Henry IV, Part I* when he says, 'I'll have a starling shall be taught to speak nothing but "Mortimer"' – he unearthed it and decided *Sturnus vulgaris*, to give the common starling its Latin name, would be the next bird to try and crack America.

In 1890 he released 60 starlings in Central Park in New York. The following year 60 more were set free in the heart of the city and Schieffelin sat back and watched.

The winged British invaders absolutely loved the States. By the late 1920s the starlings had flown as far as Mississippi and by the 1940s they had arrived in California. Today they can be found from Alaska to Florida and the population is estimated to be 200 million strong. In fact there are so many of the buggers they are now considered an invasive species and their proliferation has a major impact on native bluebird and woodpecker numbers. If birds needed Green Cards, the starlings wouldn't be picking one up anytime soon.

So Schieffelin's experiment was what we'll call a qualified success, but the tragic footnote to this strange story came in 1960, when a Lockheed Electra plane took off from Boston Airport, but hit a large flock of starlings, which caused the engines to stall and resulting in a crash that killed 62 passengers.

MERCUTIO'S FINAL DUEL

1894

The Health and Safety at Work etc. Act 1974 is a much-maligned piece of legislation. It's true that it has been variously enacted over the years to put an abrupt stop to a catalogue of seemingly innocent and safe pursuits, but danger it seems lurks everywhere, and we should all be grateful for the nanny state.

Without the timely intervention of those who enforce the Act, for example, schoolchildren in Derbyshire would have been at the mercy of malevolent mangos in 2015. Beachgoers in Yorkshire in 2011 could have been sliced asunder from the sky by deadly kites and men and women the length and breadth of the country could have bled to death had the murderous practice of securing commemorative poppies with pins not been stopped in 2003. And all those victims of 'Elf 'n' Safety are absolutely true.

A rigorous application of the Act would certainly not have gone amiss back in 1894 when an amateur dramatic group in Manchester decided to stage a production of *Romeo and Juliet*. Unfortunately Health and Safety was very much more 'optional' in those days and this lax approach was to have fatal consequences for one of the troupe. The unfortunate, budding actor in question was teenager Thomas Whalley and his appearance in the play one April evening was to be his tragic, final curtain call.

'An inquest was held yesterday at Manchester respecting

the death of Thomas William Whalley, aged 19, who was killed in an amateur dramatic performance,' reported the *Northern Daily Mail*. 'The deceased took the part of Mercutio in "Romeo and Juliet." In the duel between Mercutio and Tybalt, Mr Holmes, who represented Romeo, rushed on to separate the combatants.'

'Mr Thompson, who impersonated Tybalt, made a lunge, as required by the part, beneath Romeo's arm and unhappily his sword penetrated the chest of the deceased, who staggered and fell. He became unconscious and died soon afterwards.'

'Mr Thompson and the deceased were on the best of terms. The Coroner said it was a dangerous thing that in a mock duel people should use swords so sharp as these particular ones were. All who took part in the performance were guilty of negligence in allowing the use of such weapons.'

The poor bugger never stood a chance. 'A post mortem examination showed that a sword had penetrated his chest to a depth of seven inches [17.8cm],' wrote Carl A. Thimm in *A Complete Bibliography of Fencing and Duelling*. 'It had passed through the lung, penetrated the pericardium and had wounded the left pulmonary vein.'

Modern theatrical productions that involve swordplay are, of course, heavily regulated in the interests of Health and Safety and all the blades rendered incapable of causing serious injury to avoid a repeat of such a tragedy. This proved a major disappointment to absolutely everyone when, in 2008, Sir Fred Goodwin was cast as Brutus in an RBS production of *Julius Caesar*.

TREASURE ON THE SHELVES

1904

Objects have an uncanny knack of turning up in the strangest of places. It remains an enduring mystery, for example, how a dead giraffe turned up in the water off New York City in the 1980s or how a jar of bull's sperm was discovered sitting on the shelves of the Lost Property Office of the London Underground. Don't even ask a radiologist what kind of stuff they've discovered 'tucked away' in intimate areas of patients, it'll make your eyes water.

This particular tale of unexpected discovery concerns an extremely rare quarto copy of *Titus Andronicus*, forgotten for centuries but unearthed over 300 years later, a long, long way from home.

A quarto is a book or pamphlet produced by folding one or more printed sheets into four leaves (eight pages), with each printed page being one-quarter of the size of the full printed sheet. The earliest known printed book in Europe, believed to have been produced by Gutenberg around 1452, was a quarto.

The quarto copy in question here was printed in 1594. We know this because it bears the name of the acting company it belonged to, rather than Will's name – it was only after 1598 that Shakespeare got sole billing on quarto copies of his work – and although we have no evidence of how large the print run was, it's thought only a handful of copies were sold.

All were to be presumed lost until 1904, when our surviving original copy was unearthed in the most unlikely of locations, the home of a Swedish postal worker in the south of the country. The quarto was wrapped in a pair of eighteenth-century lottery tickets and our Scandinavian postman, not to mention a legion of bemused academics, had absolutely no idea how it had got there.

It was only dusted off and reintroduced to the world when our curious Swede read a newspaper article about the sale of an early English Bible. It had gone for a few krona and it made him think of the 'worn little English book' he had in his own collection. He was totally unaware of the Shakespeare connection but he contacted a local bookseller and the rest was history.

The news of the find was seismic in literary circles and the text immediately supplanted what had previously been the earliest printed version of *Titus Andronicus*, which dated from 1600. The discovery of the earlier, more accurate, version of the drama allowed scholars to identify and correct some of the editorial mistakes and erroneous transcriptions that had been made in the six years between 1594 and 1600.

Along with a copy of *Henry VI, Part II* published in the same year, the Swedish *Titus* is the oldest printed example of anything by Shakespeare in existence today.

The quarto edition had obviously done a few miles to make its intriguing journey to Sweden, but it was on the move again soon after it was found, when the American oil magnate and collector of Shakespeareana, Henry Clay Folger, paid over £200,000 in today's money to prise it away from our lucky postie and it is now part of the famed (if not imaginatively entitled) Folger Shakespeare Library in Washington DC.

The lesson of the story is the next time you're dusting your book shelves, be sure to check what might be hiding behind those unthumbed copies of Bill Bryson or Barbara Cartland.

JAGGARD'S STRANGEST HAT-TRICK

1911

For those of you with an attention span that exceeds that of the average MTV viewer, absent-minded goldfish or certified amnesiac, the name of William Jaggard really should ring a bell. Jaggard? Jaggard? Oh, for Christ's sake!

William Jaggard was the London publisher who flagrantly ripped Will off when he published *The Passionate Pilgrim by W. Shakespeare* in 1599. He was also the fella who subsequently helped print the fabled First Folio in 1623 and, most pertinently, he was the man it was promised would merit three separate mentions in this very book. The time has come for the third and final instalment.

This William Jaggard, however, is Captain William Jaggard who lived in Stratford-upon-Avon nearly 300 years after his namesake and who was rather an ardent admirer of the Bard. So much so in fact that in 1909 he opened 'The Shakespeare Press', a bookshop and printing business, in the town.

In 1911 he went one better in his tribute to Will when he published his *Shakespeare Bibliography*, subtitled *A Dictionary of every known issue of the writings of our National Poet and of recorded opinion thereon in the English Language*, a massive 700-page work which took him 20 painstaking years to compile.

Modern scholars accept his labour of love is an accomplished work, and in it the twentieth-century Jaggard intriguingly takes the opportunity to leap to the defence of his seventeenth-century counterpart, claiming his reputation has been unfairly tarnished by accusations of copyright infringement and that he should be remembered as the man who preserved the Shakespeare canon with the publication of the First Folio. He wrote of the first Jaggard that 'the world owes more than it deems for the safe preservation of an unparalleled literary heritage, the labour of a lifetime is gratefully dedicated.'

So were our two Jaggards related? It does seem rather an unlikely coincidence that two men separated by three centuries should share both the same name and a passion for Shakespeare, and for his part, the Stratford Jaggard consistently claimed he was a direct descendant of his namesake. The only fly in the ointment was the lack of a scrap of any documentary evidence to support his belief.

The sceptics have pointed out that a familial link and talk of the famed First Folio would probably have benefited the latter Jaggard in terms of sales of his own book. It is also worth noting that he never made the claim in print, and conspicuously not in his *Shakespeare Bibliography*, leading some to suspect that even the Captain himself wasn't all that convinced about the alleged family connection. Or, like his supposed ancestor, he was simply a bit of a chancer.

THE REHABILITATION
OF RICHARD
1924

History is littered with figures whose reputations have been tarnished by their portrayal in popular culture. Meryl Streep certainly didn't do Margaret Thatcher any favours in *The Iron Lady*, while George III was considered no less insane after Nigel Hawthorn's turn as the troubled monarch in *The Madness of King George*. King Arthur's reputation will probably never be fully repaired after Graham Chapman's performance in *Monty Python and the Holy Grail*.

Another member of this unhappy band of besmirched individuals would be Richard III, who received something of a dramatic going-over from the Bard in his play of the same name. Will did after all describe Dickie as a 'poisonous bunch-back'd toad' and his reputation as a deformed, malignant tyrant has undoubtedly endured.

Help, however, was at hand in the summer of 1924 when the Fellowship of the White Boar was formed by a Liverpool surgeon called Saxon Barton. The white boar was Richard's emblem and Barton and a small group of like-minded amateur historians had had enough of the demonisation of the king. The group was rebranded as the Richard III Society in 1959 but the quest to rehabilitate Dickie's reputation continued.

'In the belief that many features of the traditional accounts of the character and career of Richard III are neither supported by sufficient evidence nor reasonably tenable, the Society aims to promote, in every possible way, research into the life and times of Richard III, and to secure a reassessment of the material relating to this period, and of the role of this monarch in English history,' reads the mission statement of the group which boasts 4,000 members worldwide.

'The Richard III Society may, at first glance, appear to be an extraordinary phenomenon – a society dedicated to reclaiming the reputation of a king of England who died over 500 years ago and who reigned for little more than two years. Richard's infamy over the centuries has been due to the continuing popularity, and the belief in, the picture painted of *Richard III* by William Shakespeare in his play of that name. The validity of this representation of Richard has been queried over the centuries and has now been taken up by the Society.'

The whole Richard debate reached a macabre head in 2012 when his body was discovered buried beneath a car park in Leicester, dumped there unceremoniously after his death at the Battle of Bosworth in 1485. He was promptly dug up and, after an unedifying row between Leicester and York as to where the monarch should be reinterred, he was laid to rest at Leicester Cathedral in 2015.

The interesting aspect of his dramatic reappearance was the reception Richard received. Thousands flocked to witness the service, there was a slew of articles painting him in a distinctly more savoury historical light, and such was the degree of his rehabilitation in public perception that Queen Elizabeth sent a message to be read out at his burial ceremony. 'Today we recognise a King who lived through turbulent times,' penned Liz or one of her lackeys, 'and whose Christian faith sustained him in life and death.' Which is royal code for he wasn't such a bad chap really.

The Richard III Society had scored a big victory but their view was that even if the battle had been won, the war raged on and their quest to debunk Will's depiction of Dickie and have him anointed 'Best King In The World Ever' continues.

Another parallel example of historical reappraisal and a bid to undo the damage done by Shakespeare began in 2013, when a campaign was launched to redeem the reputation of the real Macbeth and move away from Will's depiction of him as a murderous figure driven by a lust for power, which ultimately led him to madness and an ignominious death by beheading. Which, we can probably all agree, isn't exactly the kind of bio you'd use on your CV.

The brainchild of MSP Alex Johnstone, the thrust of the campaign was that the real Macbeth, aka the eleventh-century Mac Bethad mac Findlaích, was in fact a benevolent ruler, the country prospered under his reign and his villainous deeds had been greatly exaggerated by the mischievous Bard for dramatic effect.

'The reign of Macbeth, set in the context of the time, was successful and outward-looking,' said Johnstone. 'To many, however, it is characterised by paranoia and murder because of Shakespeare's portrayal. The idea is not to totally discard the character created by Shakespeare, but to allow people to draw a distinction between the fictional and factual character.'

Sadly Johnstone did not elaborate on whether the *real* Macbeth was prone to making policy decisions based on witchcraft.

HITLER AND THE BARD

1926

There's an old saying that you cannot libel the dead. Many contend that's purely because there's no money in defending the deceased and should the legal profession one day discover ways of extracting cash from corpses, posthumous defamation cases will become very common indeed. The point is, once you're six feet under, it is frightfully hard to safeguard your legacy or defend your reputation.

If he weren't brown bread, the Bard would certainly agree and it is with heavy heart we must relate that one Adolf Hitler was a great admirer of Stratford's finest. Unfortunately we are talking about *that* Adolf Hitler, and whichever way you slice it, the admiration of the Führer is not something Will would have wanted from beyond the grave or otherwise.

The first evidence of Adolf's interest in Shakespeare dates back to 1926 and a notebook in which he detailed his own design for a performance of *Julius Caesar*. The Forum in Rome is depicted in a neoclassical style that became known as Nazi 'severe deco' and it's all rather ominously redolent of the Nuremberg rallies that were to follow.

Weeks after the Nazis swept to power and Hitler was appointed Chancellor, the party released an official pamphlet entitled *Shakespeare – a Germanic Writer* while at the Propaganda Ministry Rainer Schlosser, who had been given charge of the Third Reich's theatres, considered the Bard to be more German than English.

When the Second World War broke out there was a short-lived ban on the performance of Will's plays but that it was personally overturned by Hitler himself. On St George's Day the following year, as Hitler's hordes bore fought their way to the Channel ports, the Nazi elite and leading academics assembled at the National Theatre in Weimar to celebrate the 376th anniversary of Shakespeare's birth.

There were members of the Nazi party at the time who weren't as keen to extol the virtues of an Englishman while they were embroiled in a war with Blighty but Adolf was the boss and Will's detractors prudently kept schtum.

'Hitler's interest in Shakespeare had existed for some time. With characteristic loathing for what he perceived as a narrowing of German culture, particularly under the influence of the Jews, he had written in *Mein Kampf* of his desire to restore Shakespeare to his rightful place on the German stage,' wrote Irene Rima Makaryk in *Shakespeare and the Second World War: Memory, Culture, Identity.*

'Nazi aesthetics, with respect to Shakespeare in general and *The Merchant of Venice* in particular, seem ultimately to have been mediated by a recognition of Hitler's profound interest in the playwright.'

'*Coriolanus* enjoyed a firm place in the Nazi education machine throughout the Second World War, Shakespeare's text being deemed an exemplum of the virtues of the strong military leader. Examples of an understanding of Shakespeare as somehow in tune with Nazi values are unsurprising given Hitler's own evaluation of the playwright's standing in relation to German culture.'

Hitler's attempts to assimilate and appropriate the Bard were brought to an abrupt halt in 1945 when the Führer had a nasty accident with his revolver in the bunker (which, incidentally, isn't one of the solutions in the German version of *Cluedo*) and the Nazi grasp on our Will was mercifully wrestled free.

BLACK MAGIC IN LAFAYETTE

1936

One of the most famous of all Shakespearean quotes is the opening line of Macbeth's soliloquy in Act II, Scene I of the Scottish play, when our eponymous general asks, 'Is this a dagger which I see before me?' It's right up there in terms of the Bard's best one-liners, but it proved to be a question rather too close to home in 1936, when a young chap by the name of Orson Welles decided to stage a controversial version of Will's work in New York City.

It would be five years later that Welles would direct *Citizen Kane*, but before finding enduring fame and fortune with his seminal film about a dying newspaper magnate, he hit the headlines with an innovative interpretation of *Macbeth* which almost saw his career cut fatally short.

Welles' big idea was to abandon the play's traditional Scottish backdrop and set it on the Caribbean island of Haiti during the nineteenth-century slave era. The set featured a castle nestled in the jungle with stylised palm trees and skeleton imagery and he recruited a 150-strong cast exclusively made up of African American actors. The three witches became voodoo priestesses, and although he remained largely faithful to the Bard's original text, even before the curtain went up on the opening evening of Welles' production, his version had been dubbed the 'Voodoo Macbeth'.

The 1930s though were racially sensitive times in America

and certain sections of the local community near the venue, the Lafayette Theatre in Harlem, weren't happy. In particular, a group called the Harlem Communists were incensed, and believed Welles was about to stage a racist comedy that ridiculed African Americans. Angry protests outside the theatre followed and the then 20-year-old director became public enemy number one.

Things reached a dramatic head during rehearsals when Welles was accosted by an irate protestor, and although it was technically a razor rather than a dagger which was brandished, Orson suddenly saw a blade in front of him. Luck, however, was on Welles' side that day as the actor who was playing Banquo, a large gentleman by the name of Canada Lee who just happened to be a former boxer, intervened and saved Orson from a spot of impromptu street surgery.

Our Orson was unperturbed by his fortuitous escape and the public mood to the play began to change, in his own words 'for no reason at all' and by the time opening might arrived, Seventh Avenue had to be closed for ten blocks on either side as a reported 10,000 people thronged around the Lafayette Theatre in a desperate attempt to get tickets. The production went past its initial scheduled run, and proved so popular that it toured America, including a two-week stint in Texas.

Rather ironically, Welles' *Macbeth* was performed in front of segregated audiences but the director nonetheless gained widespread applause for the way he 'brought magical realism and aspects of Haitian culture to the production' as well as giving stage opportunities to black actors. *The New York Times* and the *New York Daily News* both praised the play's 'energy and excitement'.

There were though one or two dissenting voices, and critic Percy Hammond of the *Herald Tribune* criticised what he deemed the casts' inaudible and timid delivery of the Bard's lines. In response to the review, one of the African drummers involved in the production created a voodoo doll of Hammond and stuck pins in it, something Welles admitted he found funny. What was less amusing was news of Hammond's death from pneumonia at the age of 63 just 12 days after the opening night.

SNACK TIME IN STRATFORD

1963

The advent of digital sound systems has revolutionised the way sound effects are rendered in modern theatres. These days a cornucopia of frightfully realistic noises can be summoned in glorious surround sound at the mere tap of a laptop, and such is the advance in technology, directors can recreate pretty much any aural backdrop they desire.

Back in Shakespeare's day things were rather more rudimentary of course. Most of the onus fell on the actors themselves to add the required effects on stage, and while the clash of swords could be created with the collision of metal on metal in the wings, coconuts had yet to be introduced to Britain and the sound of the clip-clop of horses' hooves was but a pipe dream.

There was some specialised equipment on hand, but since the firing of a small replica cannon to emulate the sound of real artillery during an ill-fated performance of *Henry VIII* in 1613 saw The Globe burned to the ground as a result [see 'Relocation, Relocation, Relocation, 1599'], such contraptions really should have come with a health warning.

Convincingly recreating the sound of a cannon was a challenge faced by the Royal Shakespeare Company and acclaimed director Peter Hall as they prepared to stage the Wars of the Roses trilogy in Stratford-upon-Avon back in 1963. 'Elf 'n' safety precluded the use of any real pyrotechnics to make the production go with a bang and Hall and Co. were initially bereft of ideas how to get the effect just so.

Inspiration was (perhaps) on hand during a lunch break as one of the cast hungrily devoured a packet of Monster Munch. It may have been a bag of Wotsits – it doesn't really matter because this bit is all complete conjecture – but the point is Hall and Co. realised crisps were the answer they were looking for. A lackey was hastily dispatched to buy as many packets of Frazzles, Skips and Hula Hoops as petty cash would allow and the actors assembled to record the sound of inflated crisp packets being burst in lieu of cannon fire.

It was a novel solution to an age-old theatrical quandary, and by all accounts the effect was jolly effective, as the trilogy was acted out to the sound of empty bags of Golden Wonder and Walkers exploding in the background.

For those wishing to copy the RSC's clever trick however, don't bother with Pringles as the tube apparently fails to deliver the prerequisite pop.

NEVER JUDGE A BOOK
BY ITS COVER
1964

The penal system has always had an uneasy relationship with
literature. Access to books for those doing porridge is a thorny
issue, because while offenders do have rather a lot of spare time
on their hands and could probably get through *War and Peace*
in less than a week, the authorities are acutely wary of giving
criminals access to what they deem inappropriate material.
And we're not just talking about the latest Jeffrey Archer here.

Much of the acclaimed 1990s cult film *The Shawshank
Redemption*, starring Tim Robbins and Morgan Freeman,
revolved around the prisoners' attempts to build a library
and stock it with books. Freeman also led the cast in 2009 in
Invictus in which he played the late, great Nelson Mandela
and that convenient connection, as if by intelligent design,
leads us neatly into the intriguing tale of the first black
president of South Africa and Shakespeare in gaol.

It was in 1964 that Mandela was imprisoned on Robben Island
after being convicted of four counts of sabotage and conspiracy
to violently overthrow the government. He would spend the next
18 years of his life there and suffice it to say the regime was not
particularly cuddly. His reading material was severely restricted
by the South African authorities, but in 1975 the arrival of
a new prisoner by the name of Sonny Venkatrathnam saw a
surreptitious addition to the bookshelves of Robben Island.

Venkatrathnam brought in what he claimed was his Bible,
covered as it was in colourful Diwali cards celebrating the Hindu

festival of lights, and since the warden was worried about politics rather than religion, he was allowed to hold onto it. All was not as it seemed, however, and Venkatrathnam had successfully smuggled into the prison a copy of the *Complete Works of Shakespeare*.

For the next three years the book was passed around 33 of the inmates, including Mandela, and each one signed and dated their names next to particular passages that resonated with them. Mandela chose an excerpt from *Julius Caesar*, moments before the eponymous character leaves for the Senate on the Ides of March and his imminent assassination, which contains the lines: 'Cowards die many times before their deaths, The valiant never taste of death but once.'

The playwright Matthew Hahn interviewed many of the inmates before writing a play, *The Robben Island Bible*, based on events inside the notorious prison and insists Mandela's choice of the Bard's line was always intended for a wider audience.

'I believe when Nelson Mandela signed this passage, he recognized this book would get out and be circulated in the liberation movement,' he said. 'This would be the quote people looked to. It was an incredibly powerful quote and he lived his entire life according to these two lines.'

'There's this universality to Shakespeare, including many lessons on good and bad leadership, and I think Mandela found resonance in his words. He once said that "to be taken seriously as a politician, one must always quote from Shakespeare," and a lot of his speeches when he was president did just that.'

Purely coincidentally, Mandela made his mark next to that passage in *Julius Caesar* on 16 December 1977. The same day is also the date of the annual 'Reconciliation Day' in post-Apartheid South Africa, inaugurated in 1994, which would very probably never have become a reality had it not been for Mandela's vision, tenacity and compassion and, perhaps, a little literary help from the Bard.

A MERSEYSIDE MIDSUMMER

1964

The Bard and The Beatles are two of the greatest cultural exports ever to have set sail from the shores of dear old Blighty. Stratford-upon-Avon's finest and the four lads from Liverpool have conquered every corner of the planet, and even the likes of Anton Chekhov and Elvis Presley, Henrik Ibsen and Michael Jackson, can but bow down to the genius of our Will and the Fab Four

Imagine then some kind of Shakespeare-Beatles mash-up. A melding of the genius of the Bard with the combined talents of the Merseyside minstrels. A coming together of … OK you get the picture, and suffice it to say in 1964 that is exactly what happened, in the shape of a TV special called *Around the Beatles*.

Made by ITV, the variety programme opened with an image of The Globe Theatre and Ringo, dressed in hose and doublet, unfurling a flag with the name of the show on it. The action then switches to the studio and the Fab Four proceed to act out the 'play within a play', *Pyramus and Thisbe*, from Act V, Scene I of *A Midsummer Night's Dream*. The quartet play it for laughs from the start as Paul takes the Pyramus role, John is in drag as Lady Thisbe, while George plays Moonshine and Ringo is a scene-stealing Lion.

The show was broadcast in black and white in the UK in May 1964 but was shown in the States in colour in

November. Quite what an American audience made of the boys in Shakespearean costume with their thick Liverpudlian accents is intriguing.

Around the Beatles was not the only loose collaboration between the band and the Bard, and three years after the show the Fab Four released the album *Magical Mystery Tour*, which featured the 'nonsense' song *I Am The Walrus*.

By Lennon's own admission, much of the song was the result of drug taking and a desire to make a mockery of those who stubbornly tried to read hidden meaning into his lyrics. '"Walrus" is just saying a dream,' he admitted in interviews years later. 'The first line was written on one acid trip one weekend. The second line was written on the next acid trip the next weekend. The words didn't mean a lot. People draw so many conclusions and it's ridiculous. I've had tongue in cheek all along. Just because other people see depths of whatever in it. What does it really mean, "I am the Eggman?" It could have been "The pudding Basin" for all I care. It's not that serious.'

John maintained the frivolous tone right to the end of the song and this is where Shakespeare fits in. John just happened to hear a snippet from the death scene of *King Lear* on BBC Radio when he was working on 'Walrus' and liked what he heard so much that he included the spoken words at the end of the song. And so, three minutes and 52 seconds in, we hear Oswald exclaim, 'Slave, thou hast slain me. Villain, take my purse.' We later hear the exchange between Edgar and Gloucester.

There is one final Beatles and Bard connection, which came about when Paul McCartney found himself the proud owner of a cat and decided to call it Thisbe, the role Lennon had taken in their TV special. Considering the rumours about the pair's possibly turbulent relationship, read into that what you will.

'HASTA LA VISTA, BARDY'

1970

It remains one of the greatest mysteries of movie history how Arnold Schwarzenegger has never won an Academy Award. The lack of Oscars on Arnie's mantelpiece is a cinematic scandal and, if you've seen his haunting portrayal of Captain Ivan Danko in *Red Heat*, his coruscating performance as Colonel John Matrix in *Commando*, or his Major 'Dutch' Schaeffer in the seminal *Predator*, you'll be fully aware of the man's incredible range. His depiction of the thirty-eighth Governor of California was also utterly spellbinding.

OK, so Arnie is no Laurence Olivier, but if you do enjoy action-packed, testosterone-fuelled films, during which you can safely leave your brain in cold storage, he's your go-to guy. If, on the other hand, you happen to abhor witless violence, pyrotechnics that fail to disguise the absence of any discernible plot and muscle-bound Austrians with a dubious grasp of English, you can blame Mr William Shakespeare.

That's right, the Bard was unwittingly responsible for Schwarzenegger's acting career. Admittedly a chap by the name of Joe Weider must also shoulder some of the blame but Will is sadly far from blameless.

Weider was a body-building guru and Arnie's mentor. By 1970 the beefy young Austrian had already been crowned Mr Universe four times, as well as lifting (sorry) several

International Powerlifting titles, and Joe was eager to get his protégé into the movies. Cracking Hollywood was tough though and with no acting background, and a repertoire that made even Bruce Willis look versatile, Schwarzenegger struggled.

Hollywood however is nothing if not the land of pure make believe and Weider decided to gild the lily a little to help Arnie get his big break. 'He advised me on my training, on my business ventures,' Schwarzenegger admitted, 'and once, bizarrely, claimed I was a German Shakespearean actor to get me my first acting role in [a film called] *Hercules in New York,* even though I barely spoke English.'

Will's name opened doors and after his towering performance in *Hercules*, Arnie was back (sorry) in such classics as *Stay Hungry*, *The Villain* and *The Jayne Mansfield Story*.

Bizarrely Schwarzenegger actually got the chance to prove his Shakespearean credentials on camera when he starred in *Last Action Hero* in 1993, a routine blockbuster, which nonetheless features our Austrian muscle man as he parodies *Hamlet*:

ARNIE: Hey Claudius, you killed my father. Big mistake! [Grabs Claudius and throws him out of the castle window.]
VOICEOVER: Something is rotten in the state of Denmark and Hamlet is taking out the trash! No-one's going to tell this sweet prince goodnight!
ARNIE: To be or not to be? [Lights cigar, throws lighter over his shoulder.] Not to be. [Cue huge explosion which destroys the castle.]

It is every bit as excruciating as you imagine but proof of the old adage that absolutely anyone can make it in America if they work hard enough. And claim they once played Caliban in a production of *The Tempest* in Frankfurt.

WILL'S ENVELOPE
EPILOGUE
1972

The proverbial royal seal of approval has always been something coveted by courtiers and commoners alike. In the modern era such monarchical favour allows HP Foods to flog more tomato ketchup, or Proctor & Gamble to boost sales of Head & Shoulders in the form of a Royal Warrant, while there is still the unseemly yearly scramble as the annual Honours list approaches and frantic sycophants vie for the chance of getting a few letters after their name – either for services to paperclip manufacturing or, more traditionally, giving oodles of cash to the Government.

Back in the Bard's day however the royal thumbs-up was an altogether more serious business. Getting on the right side of the King or the Queen could certainly be financially beneficial in the form of a generous patronage, but angering the head on which sat the crown was ill advised and could, in extreme circumstances, result in a sudden and permanent disconnect between one's shoulders and one's bonce. We know that Elizabeth I was a generous patron of Will's work, but if we are to believe one leading Shakespearean scholar, the Bard was not as grateful for Liz's largesse as you may have imagined.

Our curious tale of regal indifference began in 1972, when two American academics discovered a poem in the notebook of a chap called Henry Stanford, a man with documented connections to the Elizabethan court. Entitled 'To the

Queen by the players', the 18-line verse was thought to have been written as a one-off epilogue for a Royal command performance of *As You Like It* given before Liz in February 1599, and there was a school of thought that the poem was penned by Will himself.

The authorship debate continued for 35 years but 'To the Queen by the players' got a scholastic boost in 2007, when Professor Jonathan Bate of the University of Warwick, and Eric Rasmussen of the University of Nevada, included the poem in their updated edition of the *RSC Complete Works of Shakespeare*, officially attributing the 18 lines to the Bard.

'This poem has been known to scholars for many years and has previously been published in an academic journal, but this is the first time it has been included in a *Complete Works*', said Professor Bate. 'Some people believe it is by Shakespeare, some people do not. I am now 99 per cent certain it was written by Shakespeare. We know from records that Shakespeare's company played at court on the day the manuscript refers to. When plays were put on at court, it was a requirement that there should be a prologue and an epilogue tailor-made for the occasion.'

With the Queen in attendance it should probably come as no seismic surprise that Will would pen a few lines for his beneficent monarch, but there is a twist in the tale according to Bate, who believes the Bard didn't exactly give the poem the time and care you'd expect given this illustrious member of the audience. 'Shakespeare was probably in the habit of dashing some lines down', he said, 'on the back of an envelope and then chucking them away.'

The more modern phrase, 'on the back of a fag packet' immediately springs to mind, and rather begs the question how Liz would have reacted had she learned of her favourite playwright's slipshod tendencies. She did, after all, have her own personal set of keys to the Tower of London and easy access to the sharpest axes in all of England.

BOGDANOV'S BRUSH WITH THE OLD BILL

1978

The police are not renowned as regular theatregoers. That is not, to be crystal clear, to cast aspersions on the cultural proclivities of the fine boys and girls in blue and what they do in their free time, but merely an acknowledgement that their professional presence is rarely required at the West End's finest dramatic establishments.

An unforeseen shortage of those little tubs of Häagen-Daz at the Lyric in 1997 did once require the hasty dispatch of two burly PCs to becalm mounting audience anger, but all in all theatres are genteel rather than riotous venues and the Old Bill are free to focus on their bread and butter of banging up MPs and hassling innocent motorists.

The Royal Shakespeare Company's production of *The Taming of the Shrew* in 1978, directed by the acclaimed Michael Bogdanov, however was very much a police matter, and proof that there's a fine line indeed between an avant-garde reimagining of the Bard's great work, and simply scaring the bejesus out of your unsuspecting audience.

Bogdanov really wanted to hammer home the play's patriarchal themes, and the misogyny *The Taming of the Shrew* is frequently accused of, and hit upon the idea of an attention-grabbing and unexpected scene before the start of the play to spice things up a bit. And so, as the houselights went down for the evening's performance, the audience witnessed a drunk sitting among them begin arguing angrily with an usherette, pushing her violently to the ground and then storming onto the stage and wrecking the ornate, contemporary Italian-style set. The inebriated and uninvited theatregoer had to be physically restrained by members of the cast and theatre employees and there was quite the commotion.

The 'drunk' was in fact the actor Jonathan Pryce, who was to play the lead role of Petruchio, and the fine actor that he is, his performance as a loutish interloper was so convincing that some of the audience had hurriedly fled the theatre to phone the police, breathlessly informing the long arm of the law that there was a madman on the loose and would they mind awfully coming over and locking him up please.

'Direct physical violence comes almost as a relief in the work of this alarming actor', read the review of Pryce's performance in the *Evening Standard*. 'What really rivets the tension is the fear of what he may do next. You know that he is confined within the role, which he delivers with fine, snarling precision, but you can never tell where those reptilian movements and spasms of murderous energy are going to stop.'

Bogdanov was delighted by the reaction to his little dramatic innovation, but slightly less pleased with himself when Her Majesty's heavies arrived mob-handed and, after learning the 'incident' they had been called to was no more than a theatrical wheeze, threatened to charge him with wasting police time.

178

DANIEL'S EARLY DEPARTURE

1989

Method actors are an intense bunch. Their immersive approach to their art takes incredible dedication and while they're not exactly renowned for being the life and soul of the party, they get results. The undisputed king of the modern method actors is Daniel Day-Lewis, a man who leaves no stone unturned in his research for a part. You don't win three Oscars just sitting on your arse. Although, come to think of it, that's exactly what he did to earn the Academy Award in 1989 for his portrayal of Christy Brown in *My Left Foot*.

Anyway, Daniel is a serious actor. He spent two weeks working in an Esso garage off the A12 in preparation for his role as avaricious oilman Daniel Plainview in *There Will Be Blood*, he joined the Harlem Crips before filming Martin Scorsese's *Gangs of New York* and he erroneously got a summer job at the Spice of India restaurant before working on *The Last of the Mohicans*. Thank God he wasn't offered the lead in *One Flew Over the Cuckoo's Nest*.

Apparently nothing, however, could prepare even him for the rigours of playing Hamlet at the National Theatre in 1989, and during one performance, Day-Lewis could no longer take the strain of playing the Dane and just walked off stage. His understudy was pressed into emergency service and Day-Lewis refused to return to the production.

Theatre land loves a gossip, the rumour mill sprang into

action and stories abounded that during the scene in which Hamlet encounters the ghost of his own father, Day-Lewis had been confronted by his own father's spectral image.

'I had a very vivid, almost hallucinatory moment in which I was engaged in a dialogue with my father,' he told *The Guardian* in 2003. 'But that wasn't the reason I had to leave the stage. I had to leave the stage because I was an empty vessel. I had nothing in me, nothing to say, nothing to give.'

He could have said his lines perhaps but the whole experience obviously had a disturbing effect on the actor and a few years later he insisted he'd hadn't in fact seen a phantom on stage. 'I may have said a lot of things in the immediate aftermath,' he said in an interview in *Time* magazine in 2012. 'If you're working in a play like *Hamlet* you explore everything through your own experience. That correspondence between father and son, or the son and the father who is no longer alive, played a huge part in that experience … but I don't remember seeing any ghosts of my father on that dreadful night.'

So 1989 was very much a mixed year for Day-Lewis, bringing as it did his first Oscar and a traumatic night at the National Theatre. It was also the year in which he was offered a part in *Ghostbusters II*, a role for which he'd already done the prep, but sadly turned down on the basis sequels are never as good as the original.

THE LIBYAN BROADCAST

1989

The great thing about being an unelected dictator is you can do and say what the hell you like. Things can become uncomfortable if you incur the ire of the international community, especially if you annoy the Americans, but tyrants do tend to have *carte blanche* domestically.

Colonel Muammar al-Gaddafi, for example, lived the life of Riley for more than four decades in Libya. Admittedly he did meet with a rather grisly end in 2011, when his political enemies caught up with him, but while he was on top he was the main man. The numero uno. The grand fromage.

Power, however, can make people do the strangest things, and in 1989 Gaddafi had a very funny turn indeed when he announced on Radio Tehran that William Shakespeare was not in fact English, but a sixteenth-century Arab Sheik by the name of Zubayr bin William. 'Sheik Zubayr', the Colonel insisted, was the genius behind *Julius Caesar*, *Much Ado About Nothing*, *et al* and he had the evidence to back it up.

The academic world was stunned. They hadn't been that gobsmacked since it was revealed Katie Price had made use of the services of a ghost writer for her seminal 2005 autobiography *Being Jordan*, but once the shock had subsided, Gaddafi's claims were quickly dismissed as a joke.

But the Colonel was not the first to try to appropriate

the Bard for the Arab world. In the nineteenth century an Ottoman scholar by the name of Ahmad Faris Shidyaq had argued that the author behind *Othello* must have possessed a detailed knowledge of Arabic culture and when you think about it, 'Sheik Zubayr' sounds like Shakespeare. A bit.

No one was quite sure whether Shidyaq was being altogether serious, but in 1960 his theory was seized upon by the historian, novelist and poet Safa Abdul-Aziz Khulusi, who wrote an article in the journal *al-Ma'rifa* ('The Knowledge'), in which he argued the Bard was absolutely, definitely of Arab extraction.

The cut of Khulusi's jib went something like this. Shakespeare used a hell of a lot of Arabic place names in his work. In *Macbeth* there is the first recorded use of the word 'assassin', which is derived from the Arabic 'ḥashshāshīyīn'. The multiple different spellings of Shakespeare's name that we have on contemporary record are evidence of English speakers struggling to come to terms with the exotic 'Sheik Zubayr'. The big finish to Khulusi's argument was his assertion that the face portrayed in the famed Chandos portrait of Shakespeare (see 'Picture Imperfect, 1856') was clearly Arabic.

The 'Shakespeare was Libyan' bandwagon, however, failed to generate much momentum despite Gadaffi's backing and the name of Sheik Zubayr was added to the already lengthy list of pretenders to the Bard's literary throne.

A few years later the Colonel famously had a cuppa with Tony Blair in a Bedouin tent outside Tripoli. Gadaffi told the PM all about his Shakespeare theory, while Blair told him Iraq had weapons of mass destruction that could be deployed in 45 minutes, and they both fell about laughing.

THE BARD
BOLDLY GOES ...

1996

The Shakespeare canon may be replete with references to astrology but allusions to the United Federation of Planets, warp drive or James T. Kirk are conspicuous by their absence. Further intensive investigation reveals absolutely no nod to phasers, set on stun or otherwise, and the Bard's quill did not once scribble any mention of an irate chap called Khan.

Strange then that the evergreen American sci-fi series *Star Trek* and spin-off film franchise should be positively teeming with references to all things Shakespearean. The show is one long, loving homage to the Bard and as early as the first series the writers were drawing on Will's work.

The ninth episode of that series, broadcast in 1966, was called 'Dagger of the Mind', a reference to Macbeth's speech in Act II, Scene I when he asks 'Or art thou but a dagger of the mind, a false creation, proceeding from the heat-oppressèd brain.' A few shows later we have an episode entitled 'The Conscience of the King', which is taken from *Hamlet*, and features a plot that revolves around a Shakespearean acting troupe and the search for a war criminal.

The Bardfest continued in *Star Trek: The Next Generation* in the 1980s, and the very first episode of the rebooted series when Captain Picard says, 'the first thing we do, let's kill all the lawyers', a line delivered by Dick in Act IV, Scene II of *Henry VI, Part II*.

In the episode 'Emergence', the android Data performs the final scene from *The Tempest* as Prospero.

And so it continues, but it is in the film franchise and *Star Trek VI: The Undiscovered Country* that we come across the most brazen borrowing from the Bard. The title itself is lifted from Hamlet's 'To be or not to be' soliloquy but it is a line from Klingon Chancellor Gorkon in the film that really interests us here. 'You have not experienced Shakespeare,' he says, 'until you have read him in the Klingon original.'

Now *Star Trek* fans are nothing if not a touch obsessive and Gorkon's assertion got them thinking. Why not translate Will into Klingon? The fact it's a fictional, made-up language didn't deter them one bit and in 1996 a hardback copy of *The Tragedy of Khamlet, Son of the Emperor of Qo'noS* was published. That's honestly true.

'For too long, readers throughout the Federation have been exposed to *The Tragedy of Khamlet, Son of the Emperor of Qo'noS*, that classic work of Klingon literature, only through inadequate and misleading English translations,' reads the blurb on the inside cover. 'Now at last, thanks to the tireless efforts of the Klingon Language Institute, this powerful drama by the legendary Klingon playwright, Wil'yam Shex'pir, can be appreciated in the elegance and glory of its original tongue.'

'This invaluable volume contains the complete text of the play, along with an English translation for easy consultation and comparison. In addition, an incisive introduction explains the play's crucial importance in Klingon culture, while copious notes illustrate how the debased English version diverges from the original, often distorting and even reversing the actual meaning of the verses.'

'*Khamlet*, the restored Klingon version, is a work that belongs in the library of every Human who hopes to truly understand what it means to be Klingon.'

The lack of native Klingon speakers (or, in real life, Klingons) meant the book didn't make the bestseller lists, but it did make the ideal Christmas gift for men in their thirties who still lived at home with their parents, and were not encumbered by hectic social lives.

Before we proceed in an orderly fashion, a brief mention of the other science fiction behemoth that is *Star Wars*. The films have not raided the Shakespearean canon in the same flagrant way *Star Trek* has, but fans of George Lucas' creation can enjoy a Bard-*Star Wars* mash-up in the form of a series of officially licensed books, such as *William Shakespeare's The Jedi Doth Return*. 'The books retell Lucas' epic *Star Wars* in the style of the immortal Bard of Avon,' enthuses the sales blurb on the website of a well-known online retailer. 'The saga of a wise (Jedi) knight and an evil (Sith) lord, of a beautiful princess held captive and a young hero coming of age, *Star Wars* abounds with all the valor and villainy of Shakespeare's greatest plays. Reimagined in glorious iambic pentameter, William Shakespeare's *Star Wars* will astound and edify learners and masters alike.'

What is even more astounding is the fact *The Jedi Doth Return* scores 4.6 out of 5 stars on the aforementioned website.

LOST PROPERTY

2000

Location, location, location, a refrain so ubiquitous in the property world it spawned its own show on Channel 4. However, it is undoubtedly sage advice for all those contemplating buying a home, but who are unsure whether the spacious four-bedroom detached house next door to the anthrax testing laboratory would be a good investment.

It is also a mantra the Shakespeare Birthplace Trust would have done well to heed in 1930 when they raided the coffers to purchase the house outside Stratford-upon-Avon in which the Bard's mother, Mary Arden, grew up. The trust really should have checked whether Mrs Arden's gaff was in the right place.

For the next 70 years tourists from far and wide visited the property as part of a wider Shakespearean pilgrimage to Stratford, but shocking news was delivered in the year 2000, when it emerged that the house had no connection whatsoever with Mary, Will or any of the family. The Shakespeare Birthplace Trust had unwittingly been involved in a mis-selling scandal on a par with PPI.

The revelation that Mary's house was no such thing was made by local historian Nat Alcock, who delved into land records and Church of England archives, which revealed that Mrs Arden had actually lived at Glebe Farm a mere 30 yards down the road from the first, false house. Remember? Location, location, location.

It was all rather embarrassing for the Shakespeare Birthplace Trust, who really ought to have been on the ball. The silver lining, however, was the fact they already owned the farmhouse now identified as the true home of Will's mater and a hasty spot of repackaging ensued as Glebe Farm was renamed Mary Arden's House.

'When the trust purchased the original house it knew perfectly well that there was no hard documentary evidence that it was the Arden family's home,' said a red-faced Roger Pringle, the Trust's director. 'It was purchased in good faith on the basis of local tradition and the guide books have always made no secret of this.'

And therein lies the rub because an investigation into how the 'false' house came to be identified as Mary's place in the late eighteenth century should have set the alarm bells ringing in the first place.

The man to make the claim of the Shakespearean connection was a local chap by the name of John Jordan. 'A self-educated wheelwright, poet, and antiquarian, born at Tiddington, near Stratford-upon-Avon,' reads his entry in *A Dictionary of Shakespeare*, 'who collected (and elaborated) anecdotes about Shakespeare and concerned himself with the Shakespeare properties. He appears to be responsible for the identification of Mary Arden's House.'

Elaborated? That's just a posh word for made up and Jordan's propensity for playing fast and loose with the Bard's legacy was not, it seems, limited to the spoken word. In fact, he was suspected of having forged Shakespeare's will and attempting to pass it off as the genuine article, and he also unsuccessfully tried to publish a document he claimed was written by the Bard's father, in which John Shakespeare confessed to his Catholic faith.

Jordan was also something of a self-styled tour guide and local amateur antiquarian and when, in 1792, he erroneously pinpointed the first house as Mary's, no one seemingly thought to question him. The tag stuck and over 200 years later the Shakespeare Birthplace Trust found itself with egg on its face, a chastening lesson in the dangers of dabbling in the property market.

STICK THAT
IN YOUR PIPE ...

2001

As we all know in these enlightened modern times, smoking is exceedingly bad for one's health. It's also detrimental to the wallet, should you fail to find one of the increasingly rare public places where you're allowed to light up and incur a £50 fine, and the disapproval of one's prurient, clean-living peers can be withering.

Back in the Bard's day though, everyone was puffing away, blissfully unaware of the potential medical consequences. Sir Walter Raleigh had recently popularised the whole tobacco-smoking vibe and much of the country was in the grip of a 40-a-day habit.

We cannot be sure whether Will was a puffer or not. The chances are the Bard probably did indulge in the odd drag but the discovery of fragments of pipes in Stratford-upon-Avon and subsequent analysis have led some to question exactly what the hell Shakespeare was smoking.

The first batch of pipes were dug up near Will's house in Stratford in 2001. They were shipped off to South Africa for testing, and after doing whatever clever bods in laboratories do, they came to the startling conclusion that whoever owned the pipes had been smoking cocaine and cannabis. 'We do not claim that any of the pipes belonged to Shakespeare himself,' admitted the lead researcher Dr Francis Thackeray. 'However we do know that some of the pipes come from the area in which he lived and they date to the 17th century.'

So was the Bard a drug fiend? The scramble for some literary evidence to back up the theory was on and it didn't take long for researchers to suggest that the 'noted weed' in Sonnet 76 was a clear reference to marijuana, while the 'journey in his head' he mentions in Sonnet 27 was the result of some hallucinogenic over-indulgence.

The Shakespeare Birthplace Trust, however, were not going to have their boy's reputation so brazenly besmirched. 'People love to come up with reasons for saying Shakespeare was not a genius,' Ann Donnelly, the curator of the Trust's museum, told *The Daily Telegraph*. 'I don't think there's any proof that he was helped in any way by taking narcotic substances. I can't say that hallucinogenic drugs were not taken, but there's no real evidence that they were. For the evidence to mean anything, I think the pipes need to come from a proper archaeological dig and to have a clear datable context.'

A fair point, Ann, and in 2015 Thackeray and his scientific chums in South Africa got their hands on some more pipe fragments. This time, however, they came not from the general Stratford environs, but from a dig in the garden of New Place, the Shakespeare family home. The boffins set to work immediately and after using a technique called, wait for it, gas chromatography–mass spectrometry, they discovered these pipes had also been used to smoke cannabis and cocaine.

The Crown Prosecution Service may have struggled to secure a conviction based on that evidence but it was certainly an intriguing revelation. Whether the Bard was out of his mind when he wrote *Julius Caesar* or *Love's Labour's Lost* is moot, but it is important to note that among the hundreds of new words Shakespeare coined for the English language, was 'addiction' (*Othello*, Act II, Scene II).

SILENCE ON STAGE

2002

'Speak the speech, I pray you, as I pronounced it to you, trippingly on the tonguc.' The Prince of Denmark's instructions to the actors ahead of the 'play within a play' in Act III, Scene II of *Hamlet*, and in a wider Shakespearean context, a reminder that the Bard's all about the spoken word. His plays, after all, were meant to be seen and heard on stage rather than simply read and studied.

Strange then that one American theatre company should decide to ignore this self-evident truth about Will's work and stage a series of his dramas without uttering a word. That's right, a Shakespeare play in which you hear not one single syllable, partial phrase or even short sentence.

The group behind this bizarre approach to performing the Bard is called Synetic Theater, and ever since they decided to stage *Hamlet* without the tedious business of actually reciting any of the original lines, the company has been pushing the boundaries with a series of silent Shakespeare shows. Or, from another perspective, they've been taking the mickey for years.

Synetic insist they convey the plot, the emotion and the dramatic tension of the plays through stylised dance, movement, acrobatics, pantomime and music. That and some rather fetching tights and Day-Glo ankle warmers.

'Since our first production in 2002, I have often been asked, without the language, is what we do really Shakespeare?'

said Paata Tsisurishvili, one of the company's founders. 'I believe it is. Since Shakespeare has been translated into multiple languages, his words having found multiple expressions and becoming a truly universal institution in the process, we believe the language of movement is a no less valid method of exploring his work than any other. As Shakespeare himself painted with words, we attempt to paint his words with our images, offering an archetypical Shakespeare that we know, as one reviewer put it, "in our bones".'

That first production was a play, which Synetic called *Hamlet ... the rest is silence*, and since then they've staged deafeningly quiet productions of *Macbeth*, *Romeo and Juliet* and *The Taming of the Shrew* among others.

There are, of course, certain advantages to going for the silent approach. Synetic have saved a small fortune over the years not having to pay a prompter and it does rather make the Bard more accessible to the aurally challenged members of the community.

The downside is that it's jolly difficult to satisfactorily portray the anguished inner conflict and state of emotional flux experienced by Hamlet during his 'To be or not to be' soliloquy if your only artistic outlet is prancing around on stage in leggings.

UNFINISHED MONKEY BUSINESS

2003

The literary canon of work written by members of the animal kingdom is pretty slim. *Me Cheeta, The Autobiography*, the story of the star of the Tarzan films of the early twentieth century, and *Bo Obama, First Dog of the United States* aside, animals have found it tough to break into the upper echelons of the publishing world.

According to the 'infinite monkey theorem' however, our furry friends could yet become literary heavyweights.

In the context of Shakespeare (he is after all the whole *raison d'être* of the book), the theory goes that if you give an infinite number of monkeys an infinite number of typewriters, one of them will eventually reproduce the Bard's complete works word for word.

The theorem is meant to illustrate the mathematics of probability, and can be applied to the works of any author, but the specific concept of a simian accidentally writing *King Lear* or *Measure for Measure* has fascinated and enraged academics in equal measure for years.

So much so that in 2003 some clever bods at the University of Plymouth decided to put the theory to the test and turned to Paignton Zoo for help. And some monkeys. The University supplied the typewriters.

Unfortunately the results were disappointing for those hoping to prove the infinite monkey theorem. Rather than recreating some of Shakespeare's finest prose, our simian cousins merely vandalised the machinery and then, well, defecated on it. They did manage to type out the letter 'S' a few times but they quickly got bored and buggered off for a banana and a bit of a scratch.

'The work was interesting but had little scientific value,' conceded the zoo's scientific officer, Dr Amy Plowman, as she cleared her desk, 'except to show that the infinite monkey theory is flawed.'

In the monkey's defence – they were Sulawesi crested macaques if you're inclined to watch David Attenborough programmes – there were serious mistakes made. Rather than an infinite number of budding simian authors, only six – Elmo, Gum, Heather, Holly, Mistletoe and Rowan, apparently – were deployed on the task and rather than being given an infinite amount of time, they were stood down after a mere month. To this day Elmo is adamant they could have cracked it if they'd only had a couple of extra weeks.

The fascination with the theorem has always endured in popular culture, and in 1987 the American playwright David Ives penned a play entitled *Words, Words, Words*, which featured three chimpanzees – Kafka, Milton and Swift – who are caged by a scientist and given typewriters. The scientist's hypothesis is that the trio will eventually write *Hamlet*.

Incidentally *Unfinished Monkey Business* was the title of the 1998 debut solo album of erstwhile Stone Roses frontman Ian Brown. Not that it's relevant.

GORE AT THE GLOBE

2006

Theatrical realism is jolly hard to achieve. Audiences are perfectly willing to suspend their collective disbelief during a performance but it remains a constant challenge for directors to realistically render a playwright's vision on stage.

Titus Andronicus is one of Shakespeare's works that has repeatedly proved such a dramatic teaser. It's the bloodiest and most violent of all of Will's *oeuvre*, featuring a grand total of 14 deaths (there are 74 fatalities in all in the Bard's plays), and short of actually committing murder on stage, directors have frequently struggled to convey the graphic horror that is central to the tale of the eponymous Roman general's merciless feud with Tamora, Queen of the Goths.

The Globe in London decided to revive the play in 2006, and drafted in director Lucy Bailey to give the production the prerequisite punch, and it is safe to say she was spectacularly successful in convincing the audience of the veracity of the gruesomeness they were witnessing

'It is a shatteringly powerful and inventive production that brilliantly captures the drama's distinctive mix of violence and sick humour', wrote *Daily Telegraph* theatre critic Charles Spencer. 'At one moment, the audience is laughing uproariously at the blackly comic glee with which Shakespeare presents his theatrical chamber of horrors; the next, it is stunned into appalled silence as it confronts the reality of suffering and cruelty ... For those with strong stomachs, this is the wildest, most darkly thrilling night in town, and one that makes you understand why Shakespeare's most notorious play was also one of his biggest box-office hits.'

In fact, Lucy was so successful with her liberal lashings of stage blood that a number of the audience actually fainted as the play unfolded, and had to be carried out. The casualties forced The Globe to issue a warning to future visitors that they 'should be aware of its graphic nature' and earned Lucy the reputation as the Quentin Tarantino of theatre land.

Whether wisely or not, the same theatre decided to stage a revival of Lucy's production in 2014 and it had evidently lost none of its ability to shock as they dropped like flies once again, five of the audience falling to the floor at the sight of Lavinia emerging on stage after being raped, her tongue cut out and her hands hacked off. Others managed to stay on their feet but were nonetheless compelled to leave the auditorium at the rather-too-realistic sight which confronted them. A spokesman conceded the show was 'not one for the squeamish' but The Globe had at least learned the lessons of 2006 and had trained first-aiders on hand to look after the impromptu fainters.

Rumours that Lucy was subsequently invited to direct a remake of *Reservoir Dogs* are completely untrue.

MACBETH
STRIPPED BARE

2007

The choice of costumes for any Shakespearean production is a vital part of the process of preparing to stage one of the Bard's plays. Some companies strive for historical accuracy and oodles of britches with their wardrobe, others opt for a contemporary, cutting-edge look (think *Romeo and Juliet* as Justin Bieber and Lady Gaga), while it will probably not be long before a particularly avant-garde and publicity hungry director stages *Much Ado About Nothing* with the entire cast dressed as astronauts.

In 2007 however, the whole 'what to wear' debate was rendered rather redundant when Spanish director José Carrasquillo decided to stage *Macbeth* over in the United States, and came to the conclusion he just couldn't be bothered to source any kilts or witches' cloaks. In fact, José couldn't be bothered with any costumes at all and so it came to pass that his *Macbeth* by the Washington Shakespeare Company was performed by an entirely naked cast.

Quickly dubbed 'Macduff in the buff' by *USA Today* and waggishly described as a 'performance stripped down to the bare essentials' by other critics, the production undeniably generated quite a buzz in theatrical circles, but it is fair to say José's decision to send his cast out onto the stage without a stitch on was not universally popular.

'Washington has decked Shakespeare out in all sorts of guises in the past six months, from dancers to orchestras to tiny ninjas', read *The Washington Post* review. 'So perhaps it's fitting that, as the festival wraps up, one company is stripping a Shakespeare work down to the bare essentials. In the current offering from Washington Shakespeare Company, a cast of intrepid actors essays a wholly uncut *Macbeth* in the nude. Not a jot of clothing is to be seen in director José Carrasquillo's staging, which is frustrating and dramatically blunt. Since much of the action is fuelled by the protagonists' concern with power and status, for instance, going the Full MacMonty lowers the stakes of the story. Clothes remain primary signifiers of an individual's place in a culture, so once apparel is cast aside, social boundaries become less clear.'

The *Metro Weekly* magazine reviewer was equally unconvinced that the Scottish play au naturel was necessarily the way forward. 'José Carrasquillo's interpretation of *Macbeth* at the Washington Shakespeare Company, a production where the full cast is nude for the entirety of the play, has most certainly gained some attention', they wrote. 'It's even inspired some chuckles – "Is that a dagger that I see before me? Oh. No. I guess it isn't". And the less said about "screwing one's courage" to any place and the pricking of thumbs the better. But the ultimate question is whether or not the idea really works. Is Carrasquillo's production a bold reimagining of Shakespeare's "Scottish Play" or a gimmick designed to lure audiences to the tough-looking Clark Street Playhouse in Crystal City? In truth, it appears to be a little of both.'

José was understandably somewhat crestfallen that his production wasn't quite the critical hit he had hoped for, but his assistant director led the defence of the play, insisting there was indeed dramatic justification for all the actors prancing around in their birthday suits. 'There is something animal-like in these people', he argued. 'They just want blood. It's about naked human ambition and José wanted to physicalise that and go all the way and show us how that works visually, orally what that might mean.'

The oral implications of the 'Macduff in the buff' really do not, well, bear thinking about.

TEENAGERS DENIED THEIR KICKS

2007

'Censorship ends in logical completeness when nobody is allowed to read any books except the books that nobody reads.'

George Bernard Shaw, *The Shewing-up of Blanco Posnet*

We have already examined how the Bard has been subject to various forms of ill-judged censorship (see 'Lear's Dramatic Suspension, 1788') in the 400 years since he shuffled off this mortal coil. Those with big ideas and a way with words often incur the wrath of those with more withered imaginations, but should he be watching from up on his celestial high, Shakespeare may well be flattered to be considered so subversive by so many.

Censorship of the Bard began in his own lifetime, but one of the most recent and most shocking examples of Shakespearean suppression was witnessed in 2007, when *Othello* was deemed unsuitable for teenagers. And we are, for the record, talking about teenagers in dear old Blighty here, the country of Will's birth, and not spotty youngsters in some far-flung, despotic backwater.

The philistines behind the belief that the tumultuous tale of the 'noble Moor', Iago and Desdemona was not appropriate for the next generation, were the Qualifications and Curriculum Authority, who deemed the play's themes of race and sexual jealousy 'too mature and sensitive' for the country's 11–14-year-olds to handle. What themes they thought 11–14-year-olds were being exposed to on *YouTube* in the privacy of their bedrooms is a mystery, but the QCA were adamant that teachers didn't want to teach *Othello* to the kids, and they recommended that one of the Bard's seminal works was removed as a set text in schools.

'Nearly all these responses [from teachers] cited one or both of two reasons', the QCA report said. 'The first was that respondents wanted to reserve this text for study at A-level. The second was that the themes and subject matter of this play are too mature and sensitive for this age group. Many respondents stated that the topic of racism was not appropriate for Key Stage 3 study and the theme of sexual jealousy was widely felt to be beyond the experience of Year 9 children. Both were subjects that respondents would not feel comfortable teaching at this level. A significant proportion also commented on the large number of sexual puns, which was felt to be a barrier to productive language analysis.'

The QCA wasn't completely anti-Shakespeare though, and deemed *Romeo and Juliet*, *A Midsummer Night's Dream*, *As You Like It* and *Julius Caesar* as suitable texts for the kiddies. So that's, respectively, plays featuring a violent death by sword and suicide, a bestial transformation, cross dressing and political assassination. They'll be having nightmares for weeks.

The QCA also wanted to ban *Topsy and Tim* titles from all Year 3 classrooms, lest the children found the book in which Tim loses his jam sandwich at the picnic too distressing, but relented when someone pointed out they'd clearly gone a bit mad.

GOING UNDERGROUND

2007

Originally created by a chap called Harry Beck back in 1931, the London Tube map is an undisputed design classic and it's rumoured to generate £3 billion annually to the economy in souvenir sales of T-shirts, mugs and assorted tat emblazoned with his iconic image. Tourists, it seems, don't actually mind being fleeced as long as Harry's map is part of the deal.

It is, of course, also jolly handy in helping to navigate the labyrinthine network of the capital's underground rail network, and although it may be an urban myth that a hapless tourist once unwisely got on the tube at Oxford Circus without a map and didn't emerge until six months later, getting about London is undoubtedly easier with Harry's famous diagram. Navigating the characters and relationships found within Shakespeare's canon could be said to be equally complex, especially if you want this entry to go any further, so stick with it.

The comparison certainly occurred to designer Kit Grover and Cambridge academic Hester Lees-Jeffries in 2007 when they were chatting about the Bard, so the pair determined to try and transpose Will's works onto Harry's template. All the lines were duly renamed so that, for example, The Northern Line became 'Warriors' line while the District Line was reinvented as 'Fathers and Daughters' and all the stations were named after Shakespearean characters, Hotspur from *Henry IV, Part I* appearing on the 'Warriors' line while King Lear and Cordelia were located on separate branches of 'Fathers and Daughters'. The way the various lines crossed each other denoted the nature of the relationships between the characters.

'Kit is an old friend and we started talking about drawing a family tree of Shakespeare characters', said Dr Lees-Jeffries. 'But when we looked at it, we thought "wouldn't a diagram in the form of the Tube map be cool?" So I came up with how the different lines might intersect. People who don't know much about Shakespeare's plays can get something from it and others who know a lot could start thinking about the development of characters.'

The Shakespeare Tube map is laden with visual gags. At the Titus (Andronicus) terminus, there is the crossed knife and fork symbol, which usually denotes food available, but in this case wryly nods to the cannibalism in the play. The classic 'Unisex' toilet symbol is placed next to the stations devoted to both Rosalind and Orlando (*As You Like It*) and Viola and Orsino (*Twelfth Night*) to indicate the sexual ambiguity in evidence in the plays, while there is a 'River Boat' sign adjacent to Ophelia (*Hamlet*), referring to her death by drowning. Richard III's stop boasts the wheelchair access symbol in acknowledgement of the references to the king's disability in the play.

If you're curious to see Kit and Hester's Shakespeare-themed map in all its Technicolor glory, a visit may well be in order to the RSC shop on the world-wide interweb, where you can purchase a mug or indeed a tea towel emblazoned with their schematic work. Now why does that idea ring a bell?

WILL IN WHITEHALL

2007

If you happen to be a fan of the classic 1980s BBC satire *Yes Minister*, not to mention its equally scathing sequel *Yes, Prime Minister*, you cannot have forgotten the character of Sir Humphrey Appleby, the ceaselessly scheming and obsequious civil servant who was so consistently duplicitous he made Judas Iscariot look like a pretty trustworthy kinda guy.

The Machiavellian government mandarin, played by the late, great Sir Nigel Hawthorne, possessed a pathological thirst for power and influence and critics have compared the character to the equally monstrously manipulative Iago in *Othello*. Admittedly, Sir Humphrey got more laughs than the man who masterminded his own master's suicide, but the point is they were both hewn from the same stone and frightfully devious.

The link between Shakespeare and the ruling elite in this case is, of course, purely literary, but in 2007 the Bard got rather closer to the top table in dear old Blighty, when Tony Blair's government announced the brightest and best civil servants around would receiving theatrical training to help improve their performance and make them far more efficient in counting paper clips. The Royal Academy of Dramatic Arts no less was to be drafted in to put the mandarins through their paces.

'Participants will receive training from RADA in business

and leadership coaching, including lessons learned from *Henry V* and *Macbeth*', read a leaked Whitehall memo, which was greedily seized upon by the press. 'The purpose is to identify a small group of senior Civil Service staff with the potential to become one of the top 200 members of the Civil Service.'

The image of the Principal Private Secretary in the Department for Environment, Food and Rural Affairs prancing around in tights is a disturbing one indeed, and even within the corridors of power at Whitehall, there were serious doubts about the proposed Shakespearean scheme.

'They will be taught how to inspire their staff by learning Shakespearean speeches and how to look less stuffy in front of television cameras', reported the *Evening Standard*. 'But the news that civil servants will be asked to recite *Henry V's* famous rally cry to his troops – "Cry God for Harry, England and St George" – prompted a sceptical response from one senior civil servant. He said: "I hope the politically correct brigade don't hear about it. It might be deemed to be religious discrimination, sexist and nationalist."'

Other, even more cynical political commentators, pointed out that the concept of adding a spot of theatre to government was nothing new whatsoever, given that Blair had been portraying himself as an honourable politician throughout the entire ten years of his stint in Downing Street, while MPs effortlessly acted like idiots every week during Prime Minister's Questions.

A CRANIAL CURIOSITY

2008

Despite the rather terminal nature of it all, dying wishes can be a funny business. People request all sorts of bizarre things done in their name after they've gone, and from Napoleon's insistence his head was shaved post mortem and the hair distributed among his friends, to the man who stipulated his wife could only inherit his £330,000 estate if she agreed to smoke five cigars a day, those not long for this mortal world frequently do the strangest things.

The celebrated Polish composer and pianist André Tchaikowsky was no different, and when he sat down to write his will in 1979, he decided to leave his body to medical science. It was a noble gesture but there was one fascinating caveat. The doctors could have his corpse 'with the exception of my skull,' he wrote, 'which shall be offered by the institution receiving my body to the Royal Shakespeare Company for use in theatrical performance.'

Sadly Tchaikowsky, who was a lifelong fan of the Bard and frequent visitor to Stratford-upon-Avon, died from cancer three years later at the age of just 46, but true to his wishes, the executors of his will ensured the RSC received his skull. Sadly, however, for the next 26 years André's cranium did little more than gather dust in a tissue-lined box in a climate-controlled room in the company's archives and he never fulfilled his post mortem wish of making it on stage.

That however finally changed in 2008 when Greg Doran directed David Tennant in *Hamlet* at the Courtyard Theatre in Stratford. The run lasted for 22 performances and unbeknownst to the audience and much of the production crew, when Tennant acted out the famed 'Alas, poor Yorick' scene in Act V, he was actually holding Tchaikowsky's skull in his hands.

'It has never been used on stage before,' said David Howells, the director of the RSC archives. 'In 1989 the actor Mark Rylance rehearsed with it for quite a while but he couldn't get past the fact it wasn't Yorick's, it was André Tchaikowsky's. That, and the fear of an accident and it being slightly macabre, was why they decided not to use it and used an exact replica.'

'You will probably have to go back to the early nineteenth century for the last time a real human skull was used in a production of *Hamlet*. Various people have known about its existence before and the director for the current production, Greg Doran, knew about it and was interested in using it. I think he wanted to make the performance as real as possible.'

News of André's long-overdue appearance in the theatre broke after the Stratford run had come to an end, but the play transferred to London and the Novello Theatre in December, and the capital was so alight with talk of the skull that Doran announced that dear old Tchaikowsky was going back into storage lest his presence detract from the rest of the performance.

It was a cunning bluff. Tennant in fact continued to clasp André's skull on stage rather than the plastic surrogate the audience had been led to believe they were watching and when the following year the BBC filmed Doran's production of *Hamlet*, Tchaikowsky was back in the spotlight and immortalised in film.

It really was what André had wanted and, after spending more than a quarter of a century stuck in a cupboard, it must have been a relief to get something of an airing. Tennant was also playing *Doctor Who* on the small screen at the same time as tackling *Hamlet*, but as far as we're aware, he spared the nation's kids sleepless nights and nightmares by landing Tchaikowsky a part in the all-conquering sci-fi series.

THE MERCHANT PROTEST

2008

The debate about whether the *Merchant of Venice* can (or should) be interpreted as a piece of anti-Semitic propaganda has been raging ever since the Bard's ink was dry on the original and enduringly contentious parchment. It is for more august tomes to wrestle with that particular religious hot potato but the literary schism it has created shows no signs of being resolved anytime soon.

The controversy reared its head once more in London in 2008, when a group of Jewish teenagers decided to make a public stand against the play, a move which led to rather unexpected consequences for their previously high-achieving school.

The educational establishment in question was the Yesodey Hatorah Senior Girls' School in Stamford Hill, north London, an area known for its large Hasidic Jewish population. Exam time was looming in the form of Key Stage 3 papers on Shakespeare for a 45-strong group of pupils, but nine of the class had a chat and decided they would not, as a matter of conscience, take the test. The paper actually featured questions on *The Tempest*, but having also studied the *Merchant of Venice* and come to the conclusion that Will was not a good egg, they opted to boycott any exam associated with his work.

Their protest saw the defiant nine score zero in that particular Key Stage 3 module, and as a result the school plunged to two-hundred and seventy-fourth in the 'valued added' educational tables, a measure of the progress made by pupils between the ages of 11 and 14. The previous year Yesodey Hatorah had proudly finished top of the pile.

There was, however, an uplifting footnote to the story. The girls' boycott may have seen their school slip down the rankings quicker than an inebriated ice skater, but their headmaster, Rabbi Pinter, resisted the temptation to stick them in detention for a year, and instead praised their moral courage.

'We felt that we needed to respect those children's views', he said. 'We did nothing to discourage them. We teach our pupils to have pride in what they believe in. If you do believe in something strongly, there can be consequences. But sometimes it's worth paying the consequences. We have never looked at them [league tables] as a goal on its own. Good results are just a by-product of what we do. When I look at Shakespeare I don't look at him as anti-Semitic. There are much better candidates for that position unfortunately.'

The Rabbi drew a line however when his Year 11s asked whether they could skip their GCSE science exams because they simply couldn't be bothered to revise.

YOOF CULTURE

2008

Engaging kids with the Bard is sometimes a Herculean task. Cultured adults such as ourselves may be fully conversant with the beauty of his iambic pentameter and acutely aware that his wit eclipses even that of Stephen Fry but let's be honest here, his language can be a tad impenetrable to the modern, callow youth, whose linguistic skills are diminished daily by technology and, in particular, texting.

Many have valiantly attempted to make the Bard 'relevant' to the yoof of the day with varying degrees of success, and one of the most recent efforts was in evidence in 2008, when a chap from Devon decided to 'translate' 15 of Will's finest works into the patois of the mean streets of modern Britain.

The author, we shall call him Martin Baum because that's his name, was inspired/foolish enough (delete according to which side of 40 you find yourself) to update the Bard in an effort to make his dramas less stuffy and, after deliberating for a nanosecond what to call his seminal tome, he opted for *To Be or Not To Be, Innit*. Lost generations of Shakespearean scholars turned simultaneously in their graves and in the process created an earthquake in the Home Counties that measured 3.2 on the Richter scale.

As Martin's title subtly suggests, *Hamlet* was one of the plays to get the treatment. He renamed the searing tale of the mental disintegration of the Prince of Denmark *Amlet* and it went something like this. "Dere was somefing minging in de

State of Denmark which was making Amlet all uncool. First, his Uncle Claudius had married his muvva, de main bitch Queen Gertrude. Then de Norwegian Fortinbras massive was freatening to invade de Danish turf and finally, and quite unexpectedly, de rank ghost of his nutty farva was spooking de crap out of him. De minging ghost told Amlet he was poisoned by Claudius and wanted him to do somefing about it. Amlet said "Aiii" and reckoned de best way was to pretend to go all loony toons to make everyone fink he was barking.'

Had enough? How about Martin's *Jools Caesar*, his reimagining of the classic tale of political manoeuvrings in Ancient Rome. 'Jools Caesar was de man with de plan in de Roman massive. Getting maximum respect for mashing de minging Gauls and de Pompey warriors. Even his bro Mark Antney fought he was de main man.'

Quite. Academic circles were of course appalled at what they claimed was his desecration of the Bard, but Martin was quick to leap to his own defence, chiefly because no one else would. 'I intended it for adults but at my son's school the children seem to really enjoy it and the publisher has had feedback to say it is popular among youngsters', he said. 'Anything that introduces children to Shakespeare I think is a good thing. And if it turns them on to reading, that's great. This suggestion of dumbing down Shakespeare really amused me. I am a writer and satirist and I love the classics and decided to rewrite some of Shakespeare's plays. Next up, I want to give Charles Dickens a good seeing to, if you know what I mean.'

Depending entirely on your point of view, our Martin was mercilessly/mercifully true to his word and in 2010 *Oi, Mate, Gimme Some More!* hit the shelves. His next, eagerly anticipated project is (perhaps) a reworking of William Wordsworth's collected poems: 'I was walkin without me mates, all on my lonesome like I was in da cloudy hills or somefing, when I spotted a big bunch of flowers, which were all like, well, yellow.'

DUFFY'S POETIC DING-DONG

2008

It has been a long time since Shakespeare personally courted controversy, whether intentionally or not. He has, after all, been dead for four centuries and while his work has repeatedly been the catalyst for contention over the years, the fault does not lie with the Bard himself. Did we mention he's an ex-playwright these days? It's jolly hard to be deliberately inflammatory when you're six feet under.

A relatively recent and high-profile incident of Will being dragged into a fight that was not of his own making came in 2008, when the acclaimed poet and playwright, Carol Ann Duffy, was rather miffed when one her poems – 'Education for Leisure' – was pulled from the GCSE curriculum by educational bigwigs.

The unceremonious removal of the 1985 poem was the result of a complaint by a teacher called Pat Schofield from Leicestershire, who was concerned the content was rather too potentially murderous and violent for 16-year-olds to be studying and dismissed it as 'absolutely horrendous'. It begins with the line 'Today I am going to kill something' and concludes with the anonymous narrator heading out of the house brandishing a bread knife. The rest is left to the imagination and there is even a reference to the Bard in the poem:

I squash a fly against the window with my thumb.
We did that at school. Shakespeare. It was in
another language and now the fly is in another language.
I breathe out talent on the glass to write my name.

To say Carol was unhappy with her piece's educational exile would be an understatement, not least because the entire anthology in which it originally appeared was also pulled from classrooms. She was ruddy furious and responded in the best way she knew how, penning a new poem, sarcastically entitled 'Mrs Schofield's GCSE', in which she parodied an English exam paper, and quite reasonably pointed out that Will's work remained on the curriculum despite being absolutely riddled with knives and daggers, murderous thoughts and, you know, lots of stabbing. It went like this:

You must prepare your bosom for his knife,
said Portia to Antonio in which
of Shakespeare's Comedies? Who killed his wife,
insane with jealousy? And which Scots witch
knew Something wicked this way comes? Who said
Is this a dagger which I see? Which Tragedy?
Whose blade was drawn which led to Tybalt's death?
To whom did dying Caesar say Et tu? And why?
Something is rotten in the state of Denmark – do you
know what this means? Explain how poetry
pursues the human like the smitten moon
above the weeping, laughing earth; how we
make prayers of it. Nothing will come of nothing:
speak again. Said by which King? You may begin.

Shakespeare must have been sorely tempted to scream 'leave it, she's not worth it', but was unable to do so on account of being dead.

The row, however, didn't do Carol's career any undue

harm and the following year she succeeded Andrew Motion as the Poet Laureate, the first woman to hold the position. Her appointment was officially confirmed after a private audience with the Queen, a meeting which only took place after Carol had presumably been thoroughly patted down for concealed weapons and passed through a barrage of metal detectors.

SOZZLED ON STAGE

2010

Actors have always revelled in their reputation as bon viveurs. The tendency of those who tread the boards to indulge in a tipple or ten once the final curtain has come down is legendary and those in the theatrical profession love nothing more than dissecting the genius of their latest performance over a large glass of something red. Or maybe white.

More seasoned performers are not averse to a little livener *before* venturing onto the stage, just to get the creative juices flowing you understand and guard against stage fright, but the golden rule is everything in moderation as it is jolly hard to successfully deliver Gloucester's soliloquy in *Henry VI, Part III* – the longest monologue in the Bard's canon – if you're three sheets to the wind.

'The Shit-Faced Shakespeare' company (if you'll pardon our French), however, beg to differ and ever since 2010 the touring troupe of actors have been performing Will's work with one of their number very deliberately and very much under the influence in front of their audience.

Intentionally sending out an inebriated actor is certainly a novel approach to Shakespeare, and while the cynics among you may dismiss the ploy as a cheap stunt, the company insist they're not just playing it for laughs. 'We're seeking to introduce a new generation of theatregoers to the works of the Bard', proclaims their website, 'by reviving the raucous, interactive and vibrant nature of Elizabethan theatre with a very modern twist – reminding them as we go to always enjoy Shakespeare responsibly.'

The 'interactive' element revolves around members of the audience being asked to call for the evening's sozzled performer to be replaced if they're slurring their lines or demanding they drink more if they're proving disappointingly lucid and although Shakespeare on the sauce may not be everyone's cup of tea, the show has proved successful, finishing as runner-up in the 'Best Comedy' category at the Brighton Fringe in 2013. Two years later the company exported the show across the Atlantic as a franchise when it premièred in Boston.

'We get one of the cast highly drunk four hours before – it's a low and slow affair, at their leisure – then send them on stage to sink or swim', explained director Lewis Ironside. 'The rest of the cast members are stone cold sober. They normally swim but sometimes they sink and it's funny.'

'It's just incredibly fun. Everyone plays multiple roles, the cast drinks on rotation, meaning you do one a fortnight. It's got a never-ending appeal for us to perform because it's never the same.

'We do look after the actors. They're never left alone and we have a compere in every single show. It's a very interactive form of theatre, but we always make sure it's strictly compered to make sure the drunk never goes too far off the rails.'

The libatious troupe have performed a wide range of the Bard's plays from *A Midsummer's Night Dram* to *Love's Labour Sloshed, The Tempissed* to *The Very Merry Wives of Windsor*, but their searing staging of *Antonic and Cleoportra* remains their most celebrated show.

A FATAL
FAMILY TRAGEDY

2011

Nobody does tragedy quite like our Will. The Bard's ability
to pluck at his audience's heartstrings is remarkable, and
although some of his drama resembles a theatrical version
of a Quentin Tarantino film in terms of the final body count,
he rarely fails to extract a tear as he kills off yet another one
of his characters.

One of the most famous of all the deaths in the
Shakespearean canon is that of Ophelia in *Hamlet*, a
harrowing tale of a young woman driven to madness by
the death of her father and then to an early grave after
she drowns in a stream, falling into the water with her
floral garlands of 'crow-flowers, nettles, daisies and long
purples'. Suicide or not, it's an unpleasant way to go and
further evidence of the Bard's penchant for a grisly demise.

Hamlet of course is set in Denmark, but a discovery
made in 2011 suggested that Will may have drawn macabre
inspiration for the Ophelia storyline rather closer to home,
and that her death could have actually been a retelling of
the fate of one of Shakespeare's own relatives.

The claim was made by academics from Oxford University
after trawling through Tudor coroners' reports into
accidental deaths as part of a four-year project to establish
why they never got invited to parties. Or maybe it wasn't.
Anyway, among all the unpalatable tales of unplanned
demises, they came across the case of a young child who had

drowned in a river just 20 miles (32.2km) from Stratford-upon-Avon in the sixteenth century.

'By reason of collecting and holding out certain flowers,' wrote the coroner, 'called "yelowe boddles" growing on the bank of a certain small channel at Upton aforesaid called Upton myll pond – the same Jane Shaxspere the said sixteenth day of June about the eighth hour after noon of the same day suddenly and by misfortune fell into the same small channel and was drowned in the aforesaid small channel; and then and there she instantly died. And thus the aforesaid flowers were the cause of the death of the aforesaid Jane; and they are worth nothing.'

OK, so we have a Jane Shaxspere who drowned collecting flowers. Ophelia drowned surrounded by flowers. Coincidence, or drama drawn from real life?

We have already learned how Shakespeare's name was spelt in a myriad of different ways in his own era, so it is perfectly plausible that poor Jane Shaxspere was a member of another branch of the Shakespeare family, just down the road from Stratford. It's true Will was just five when the tragedy occurred in 1569, but if they did share the same DNA, it's unlikely he would forget the event in a hurry.

'Even if Jane Shaxspere were not related to the playwright, the echo of their names might well have meant that this story stuck in his mind,' argued Emma Smith of Oxford University's English language and literature faculty. 'It's a good reminder that while Shakespeare's plays draw on well-attested literary sources, they also often have roots in gossip, the mundane, and the domestic detail of everyday life.'

Not for the first time when we come to contemplate the Bard's sources and inspiration, we may never know definitively whether Ophelia was a literary nod to a dead relative 30 years after the event or not. Similarly we shall forever be in the dark about the impact on Will in his youth when he found a discarded coin and innocently asked his mother, '2p or not 2p?'

VERONA'S
FAUX TOURIST TRAP

2012

There are many rivals for the title of the most famous scene in all of Shakespeare. The Prince of Denmark's 'To be or not to be' soliloquy in *Hamlet* is, of course, a perennial frontrunner, while the slaying of Julius Caesar at the forum or Macbeth's encounter with the three witches are as famous as they are finely scripted.

Another heavyweight contender is the famed balcony scene in *Romeo and Juliet* when the two young lovers in Verona profess their love for each other and their pledge to marry. In terms of romantic classics, it blows the socks off anything Leo and Kate conjured up on screen in *Titanic*.

The enduring resonance of the scene is evidenced in modern-day Verona as thousands of tourists flock each year to the city, and in particular a beautiful thirteenth-century house named Casa di Giulietta ('Juliet's house'), which just happens to boast an ornate stone balcony overlooking a medieval courtyard. Ring any bells?

Young couples can't get enough of the attraction but the tradition of sticking notes declaring their amorous devotion for each other on the wall beneath the balcony has played havoc with the architecture, most opting for a piece of chewing gum to achieve that elusive adhesiveness, with the result that, in 2012, the exasperated local authorities introduced a €500 fine for anyone caught gumming up the ancient wall.

This though is merely the prelude to our tale, because when you think about it, the claim of 'Juliet's balcony' to have any Shakespearean connection whatsoever is as spurious as, say, a cosmetics firm that insists a tube of £30 cream can stop you ageing.

Firstly Romeo and Juliet weren't *real*. Juliet never stood on the balcony. Because. She. Didn't. Exist. The Italian equivalent of the Verona Tourist Board (let's call it the VTB) has got this one covered though, countering that, yes, she's fictitious, but it's probably the balcony that *inspired* Will to write the scene. Really? The same Will who, as far as we know, never got as far as Calais let alone Verona?

At this point the VTB usually gets quite irate but we haven't even touched upon the most damning piece of evidence yet, namely that Shakespeare didn't even write a balcony scene between the 'star-cross'd lovers' in the first place. Take that, VTB.

If you grab a copy of the play, Act II, Scene II begins with Romeo's line, 'He jests at scars that never felt a wound.' This is followed by the stage direction, 'Juliet appears above at window', and Romeo continues, 'But soft, what light through yonder window breaks?'

The word balcony is conspicuous by its absence, and to further confuse matters *The Oxford English Dictionary* dates the first recorded reference to a 'balcone' to 1618, two years after the Bard had popped his clogs. Add to that Shakespeare's source material for the play, Arthur Brooke's 1562 poem *Romeus and Juliet*, also alludes only to 'within her window, and anon the Moone did shine so bright, That she espyde her love.' So how has the scene become synonymous with a bloody balcony?

The answer lies with another playwright called Thomas Otway, who wrote a drama called *The History and Fall of Caius Marius*, published in 1679, which, ahem, liberally 'borrowed' dialogue, characters and plot from *Romeo and Juliet*. In his work Otway pens a scene between 'his' young lovers Marius and Lavinia (who even says 'O Marius, Marius! Wherefore are thou Marius?') and he does indeed mention a balcony in his stage directions.

The History and Fall of Caius Marius was popular, and between 1701 and 1735, it was staged over 30 times in London alone. The balcony slowly became synonymous with the romantic scene and when *Romeo and Juliet* regained popularity with audiences in the second half of the eighteenth century, they 'inherited' the balcony iconography. The deal was sealed in 1759 when a famous etching of a performance of *Romeo and Juliet* in Covent Garden was made featuring Juliet looking down from a prop balcony to her onstage Romeo.

So the VTB can bluster all they like but their balcony in Verona, as pretty (and profitable) as it is, has no tenable connection to Will whatsoever. An accusation that could also be levelled at the Isle of Wight after it claimed to have been the inspiration for the setting of *The Tempest*. Everybody knows the Isle of Wight wasn't discovered until 1908.

HARBURGH'S UNLIKELY NOD TO THE BARD

2013

Sporting types are not renowned as intellectual heavyweights. It's probably a cruel stereotype, but there remains a lingering belief that those who are adept enough to earn their living courtesy of their physical prowess spend more time exercising their bodies than their minds. One suspects, for example, that Wayne Rooney spends his considerable spare time watching the *Real Housewives of Cheshire* rather than flicking through *War and Peace* while it's a safe bet Lewis Hamilton isn't a lifetime member of the Friends of the Tate Modern.

We must, then, head across the Atlantic and pay a visit to our American cousins for a rare example of a sporting intellectual and the intriguing tale of the American Football coach with a penchant for surreptitiously quoting the Bard. The man in question is Jim Harburgh, who was a former National Football League quarterback and, between 2011 and 2014, the head coach of the famous San Francisco 49ers.

It was in 2013, however, that Jim revealed his hitherto secret literary bent when he was asked in a pre-match press conference what had been the hardest hit he had ever experienced as a player. At first Jim insisted he did not remember but when pressed, he replied thus.

'I got some scars', he told the assembled members of the media. 'Sometime I'll have you over for a barbecue and I'll strip my sleeves and show my scars. I usually do it about once a year for my neighbours. Feast my neighbours and talk about days gone by. But today's not the day. You will be included for the yearly barbecue.'

The sports hacks departed thinking Jim had lost the plot but one bright spark thought his quotes sounded familiar and suggested the 49ers head coach was in fact cleverly paraphrasing the Saint Crispin's Day speech from Act IV, Scene III of *Henry V*. Which, in case you have forgotten, goes exactly like this:

Will yearly on the vigil feast his neighbours
And say, 'To-morrow is Saint Crispian.'
Then will he strip his sleeve and show his scars,
And say, 'These wounds I had on Crispin's day.'
Old men forget; yet all shall be forgot
But he'll remember with advantages
What feats he did that day.

The press had to rapidly reassess their opinion of Jim and it transpired his deft nod to the Bard was not the first time he had referenced Shakespeare. A quick check of the notes revealed earlier in the year he'd been at it in the build-up to the annual Super Bowl, responding to a question from a reporter about his team. 'The thing I also think about is the San Francisco 49ers, our players, they're my brothers', he replied. 'For he who sheds blood with me shall also be my brother.' The original quote from *Henry V* is 'For he to-day that sheds his blood with me shall be my brother.'

Sadly Jim's unlikely but superb Shakespeare-themed press conferences came to an unscheduled end in 2014 when he lost his job with the 49ers, bringing to an ironic halt to his plans to weave in a quote from *All's Well That Ends Well* at his next meeting with the media.

AN OVINE ODDITY
2014

Shakespeare liked sheep. Nobody is suggesting anything untoward or unseemly you understand, but the Bard's work is replete with ovine references, and pick up any of his plays and you won't have to read for too long before happening upon some mention of our woolly friends.

In the drama that bears his name, *Henry VI* refers to 'shepherds looking on their silly sheep', Prince Arthur in *King John* insists 'So I were out of prison and kept sheep, I should be as merry as the day is long', while the shepherd Corin in *As You Like It* insists 'the greatest of my pride is to see my ewes graze and my lambs suck'.

There are discussions of the price of sheep and their fleeces in both *Henry IV, Part II* and *The Winter's Tale,* comic dialogue about shepherds and their flocks in *The Two Gentlemen of Verona*, while in *Henry VIII* the king and his followers disguise themselves as shepherds. Yep, Will was fond indeed of his literary nods to lambs, ewes and rams.

That said it must remain a point of debate whether the Bard would have approved an ovine-inspired retelling of one of his greatest works or, to give it its proper title, *King Lear with Sheep*. Yes, the tragedy of the monarch turned mad and a kingdom split asunder retold on a stage populated by sheep. To be fair, there is one human actor in the mix but sheep are very much the dominant theme here.

King Lear with Sheep was first performed on a farm in

Sussex in 2014 but audiences unsurprisingly needed some help with the whole premise of the production. 'There's a director whose cast are late to perform *King Lear*,' explained director Missouri Williams. 'So he has to go on and apologise for his actors. Then when they arrive they don't perform and ignore him. It never occurs to him that they are sheep and obviously can't perform *King Lear*. So he has a nervous breakdown and starts performing the play himself.'

Theatre critics were like moths to a flame to see such an unusual play and to be fair, *King Lear with Sheep* seemed to go down rather well. 'The piece is exactly what it says on the tin and I can safely say that I will never see anything remotely like it again in a hurry,' wrote Paul Taylor in *The Independent*. 'It is, by turns, funny, charming, bonkers, delicate, barking (or baa-ing), poetic, challenging and faintly smelly. It throws Shakespeare and sheep (that ineluctable binary) into fresh and arresting relief. You will never feel about either of them in quite the same way. Never pulling the wool over your eyes, this uncategorisable delight give you much to, erm, ruminate upon.'

'It's deliriously absurd and haunting. Is this man an egomaniac nutter or has his egotism had a weird Kafka-esque effect? ... instead of waking up to find himself turned [into] a cockroach, he struggles to the realisation that emotional neglect has turned his entire court into unreciprocating sheep.'

Crikey. Who knew ovine actors were so powerful on stage? *King Lear with Sheep* transferred to the Courtyard Theatre in London in 2015 but it does raise the question of where the hell the cast stayed for the duration of the run.

Another equally bizarre, animal-themed reimagining of Shakespeare was also on show in 2015 after a chap called Kevin Broccoli decided what the world was really waiting for was a production of *Hamlet* brought to life by pugs. You know, the small dogs with downcast faces that make them look like miserable OAPs.

'I want to produce the first-ever, all-pug production of *Hamlet*,' Broccoli explained. 'The plan is to have the pug actors directed on stage by their handlers or owners. Meanwhile, human actors will read their lines off to the side of the stage.'

Genius. Broccoli cunningly dubbed his project *Pug-Let* and turned to crowdfunding on social media to raise the readies. Remarkably nearly 200 poor deluded fools between them pledged $5,000 (obviously this had to be in the States) and *Pug-Let* was good to go.

A one-off performance was duly scheduled but tickets sold like hot cakes and Broccoli had to turn to new media once again for a solution. 'I have over 4,000 e-mails from people who can't go,' he said, 'asking if they can see it on live stream.' Which proves once again that some people really will watch absolutely anything online.

WILL CONQUERS POLAND

2014

The Bard's global reach is undisputed. In 2012, for example, all 37 of Will's plays were performed at The Globe in 37 languages, from Urdu to Swahili to Turkish, by acting companies from six continents and countries as diverse as China and South Sudan. *Othello* has been staged at the White House in Washington DC while The Globe Theatre Company took a production of *Hamlet* to North Korea.

His worldwide appeal was further underlined in 2014, when The Shakespeare Theatre in the Polish city of Gdansk was officially opened, the intriguing culmination of nearly 25 years of work by local academics to commemorate an intriguing historic link between the Bard and the Baltic port. The inauguration of the theatre was no modern attempt to cash in on Will's enduring popularity but rather a nod to the acting troupes from Britain who were regular visitors to the city some 400 years earlier to perform Shakespeare's dramas.

'The idea of having a Shakespearean theatre in Gdansk is not out of the blue, it has strong historical backing,' Professor Jerzy Limon, the theatre's director, told the BBC. 'English actors first came to Gdansk in 1601. They kept coming for over half a century and Shakespeare's plays were performed here during his lifetime.'

'Rock music is today's most conspicuous example of British cultural presence worldwide. But it started long ago with these companies that toured the continent and came to Gdansk almost every summer.'

'In one of the surviving documents the author says the English [actors] were followed by virgins who travelled from one town to another … Shakespeare always reminds us how much we have in common because the language he uses and the problems he describes are universal.'

In the early seventeenth century Gdansk had one of the largest English-speaking communities on the continent. By 1610, however, the majority of the performances were in German, the city's *lingua franca*. Productions were staged in a wooden playhouse called the Fencing School, which, when it wasn't populated by thespian types, also hosted fencing classes and bear baiting.

The Shakespeare Theatre is built where the Fencing School once stood and the original plan was to follow the template of The Globe and construct an open-air venue until it was pointed out the winters in Gdansk were bloody freezing and Limon and Co. agreed to install a 90-ton retractable roof to allow *al fresco* performances when the elements permitted.

Limon began planning his ambitious endeavour in 1990 but initially hit something of a brick wall in terms of fundraising. Things looked bleak but a speculative letter to Prince Charles, who agreed to become patron of the project, got things moving again. 'In my 25 years' experience of dealing with all circles of society he is the only person so far who responded to a letter from a nobody,' the professor said.

Poland joined the EU in 2004, which really got the money moving in the form of grants from Brussels, and construction finally began in 2011. The EU of course has countless vociferous critics, but if the beleaguered British tax payer knew some of their cash was going to help export the Bard in such ways, UKIP would go into electoral meltdown overnight.

THE MYSTERY OF THE BARD'S DICTIONARY

2014

Had he not joined the choir invisible more than 300 years before the game was invented, Shakespeare would definitely have been a contender for the crown of world's greatest *Scrabble* player. The Bard had a big vocabulary to say the least, and such was the largesse of his lexicon that the acclaimed Shakespearean professor, Louis Marder, once wrote that he 'was so facile in employing words that he was able to use over 7,000 of them – more than occur in the whole King James Version of the Bible – only once and never again.'

Shakespeare's linguistic capacity has long fascinated scholars and so it was with understandable excitement the literary world greeted the claim, in 2014, that a couple of American booksellers had unearthed the Bard's very own, personal dictionary. If true, the find would have made Hitler's diaries or Napoleon's shopping list look like historical bric-a-brac.

The book in question was John Baret's *Alvearie or Quadruple Dictionarie*, published in London in 1580. It was not strictly a dictionary in the modern sense of defining words, but more a guide to the French, Latin and Greek translations of English words with accompanying expressions to add some context, but it was nonetheless the go-to reference title for Elizabethan linguistics.

Our American friends bought the book on eBay in 2008 for

£2,750, and after six years of meticulously studying the text they went public, confidently asserting it had once belonged to Will himself. The handwritten notes in the margin, they cried, the phrases that appeared in both *Alvearie* and the Bard's plays, they added, all proved they had come into possession of Will's dictionary.

'Over the course of discovery, it became impossible for us to neglect a host of personal markers that run throughout the annotated book', the booksellers wrote on their website, 'fingerprints left by the annotator that reveal a personality and hint at an identity ... there are idiosyncratic renderings by the annotator of the letters "W" and "S". In addition, there is a preponderance of natural history annotations, interest in the language of clothing and costume of the period critical to stagecraft, and annotations that connect with our understanding of Shakespeare's father and his profession.'

George Koppelman, one half of our bibliophile duo, went further. 'I looked at an annotation, "drought in summer"', he said. 'And my first thought was that it sounded like a poetic fragment. And then I looked it up and I found that "drought in summer" was basically used as "summer's drought" in *Titus Andronicus*. Later, we realized that "summer" is a very, very common word in Shakespeare – he must have used it a hundred times – but "drought" only one time.'

It was certainly a detailed argument, but the experts at the Folger Shakespeare Library in Washington remained unconvinced of the authenticity of the discovery. 'Even the most sceptical scholar would be thrilled to find a new piece of documentary evidence about William Shakespeare', the Library conceded. 'Scholars, however, will only support the identification of Shakespeare as annotator if they feel it would be *unreasonable to doubt* that identification. This is a fairly high evidentiary standard, since it requires one to treat sceptically the idea that this handwriting is Shakespeare's and to seek out counterexamples that might prove it false.'

Other scholars pointed out the reason that Baret and Shakespeare seemed to speak a common language was because, durr, they did speak a common language. They were roughly contemporaries, they were both English and they both earned a crust as writers. It's not rocket science, is it?

At the time of going to press, the provenance of the *Alvearie* had still not been conclusively established either way, but we should point out that Koppelman and his chum's unwavering conviction that the book did once sit proudly on the shelves of Shakespeare's office has nothing whatsoever, no sirce, to do with its estimated resale price of £70million, should it prove to be the real deal. They had never given that a moment's thought.

ROLE REVERSAL
DOWN UNDER

2014

Theatre land generally frowns upon members of the audience on the stage. If it happens to be an excited seven-year-old meeting Widow Twankey during a matinee of *Aladdin,* that's not a problem, but Shakespeare is not panto and those who come to see the Bard's work dramatised are actively encouraged not to encroach onto the actor's arena.

Unless that is you happened to purchase a ticket for the Sydney Theatre Company's production of *Macbeth* in 2014, when you would have found yourself in the surreal situation of sitting on the aforementioned stage, watching the cast of the Scottish play do their dramatic thing in the empty stalls.

The unusual theatrical role reversal was the brainchild of director Kip Williams and set designer Alice Babidge, and saw theatregoers Down Under positioned in temporary chairs on the boards, while the actors took up residence in the traditional seating area.

'The social and political world [of the play] is reflected in the unusual staging', read the review in *The Australian* newspaper. 'Kip Williams and Alice Babidge cram a reduced audience on to the stage of the Sydney Theatre, with a large playing space on the floor of the stalls and the vast auditorium looming behind. The emptiness of all those serried rows of seats, in the context of this story, is chilling. They become the setting for several scenes of exile.'

The innovative production did, however, pose a number

of logistical problems, not least the emphasis it put on the audience ensuring they turned up on time. 'This is *Macbeth* like you have never seen it before', declared the Sydney Theatre Company's website. 'Patrons in possession of tickets to this sold out production should come expecting a memorable theatre experience. Due to the non-conventional staging design and close proximity between the audience and performers, latecomers will not be able to enter the theatre after the performance has commenced.'

The proximity was also a bit of a problem. Macbeth boasts more than its fair share of grisly murders and the company had to significantly reduce the volume of fake blood it used to ensure the front row of the audience did not go home drenched in claret. 'There's a lot of killing', admitted Babidge, 'but I feel like we've been incredibly, incredibly plain in our use of blood.'

The theatre's accountants weren't happy either. The rejigging of the dramatic space saw the audience capacity plummet from 896 to just 360, but ticket prices were unchanged and as they bashed anxiously away at their calculators and tweaked their spreadsheets, the bean counters were horrified to realise they might not get their Christmas bonuses.

Critically however this back-to-front *Macbeth* was a resounding success and evidence that all the world, including the front row, aisles and even the upper circle at a pinch, can indeed be a stage.

THE ERRORS IN EXAMINATION

2014

Studying Shakespeare is a rite of passage for every child in the country at some stage of their academic careers. In fact it's the law, and although there are no recorded incidents yet of a teenager being banged up for failing to hand in an essay on the politics of *Henry V*, since 2014 the nation's next generation have been expected to get acquainted more intimately than ever with Will's dramatic works.

'All pupils will be required to learn at least two of the Bard's plays in full between the age of 11 and 14 – up from one at the moment – as part of a wide-ranging plan to drive up education standards', reported *The Daily Telegraph*. 'The move follows criticism of the existing curriculum amid claims pupils can leave school without studying anything more than bite-sized extracts of Shakespeare's most famous plays such as *Hamlet*, *Macbeth*, *King Lear*, *Othello* and *Romeo and Juliet*.'

The drive to place the Bard at the forefront of an educational revolution is of course to be applauded, but judging by some of the woefully misguided answers supplied by students in their Shakespearean exams that are poised to follow, the revolution might take a little while to materialise.

'The greatest writer of the Renaissance was William Shakespeare', began one GCSE candidate in their all-important paper. 'He was born in the year 1564, supposedly on his birthday. He never made much money and is famous only because of his plays. He wrote tragedies, comedies, and hysterectomies, all in Islamic pentameter. Romeo and Juliet are an example of a heroic couplet.'

Another ventured the Fool's remark in *King Lear* 'that thou madest thy daughters thy mothers; for ... thou gavest them the rod and puttest down thine own breeches', meant 'King Lear pulled down his trousers and gave his daughters the rod.' In a similarly saucy vein, one student argued, 'it is mainly Hamlet's actions that lead people to believe him mad – appearing and frightening Ophelia in her bedroom with his trousers round his ankles.'

Will's marital status has also proved another point of inadvertent comic confusion. 'Shakespeare married Anne Hathaway', ventured one student, 'but he mostly lived at Windsor with his merry wives. This is quite usual with actors.'

Other Shakespearean howlers include the pupil who was convinced the Bard had been indulging in the wacky baccy and the witches in *Macbeth* were merely a hallucination. 'Macbeth had been smoking up', they wrote, 'and imagined them all.' Another interesting theory on the Scottish play was 'Lady Macbeth had a desire to have Macbeth on the throne so she "asked him to show her his manhood".'

Other flustered examinees have asserted that Juliet's mother was 'Lady Copulate', that 'Cleopatra killed herself by taking aspic and died in her needle' and '*Antony and Cleopatra* is full of phallic cymbals.' A striking example of historic revisionism meanwhile maintained that 'as a youth Shakespeare spent a year under Queen Elizabeth'.

It is enough to make the education profession weep, and if further proof was required of students' struggles to get to grips with the Bard, it is provided by the hapless pupil who hilariously got their Leonardo DiCaprio films rather mixed up and concluded that Romeo died on the *Titanic*.

THE DIGITAL CONDUCTOR
2014

If there's one thing the modern world seems to cherish above almost all else, it's interactivity. Back in the day, that merely meant you were occasionally allowed to touch stuff in a museum or encouraged to write a letter in response to a televisual programme, but today if you can't share your innermost and utterly inane thoughts about 'an event' a nanosecond after it has happened, it just ain't worth doing.

In ye olde Shakespearean times, interactivity was rudimentary. If the audience liked the Bard's latest blockbuster, they'd clap and cheer, and if they did not, they'd boo. If they thought Will had really suffered a dramatic swing and a miss, the actors could expect a barrage of fruity language, a few flying turnips and a potential riot.

That of course just won't do in the era of Twitter, Facebook *et al*, and in 2014 audience interaction with the Bard was dragged kicking and screaming into the twenty-first century, when the Victoria and Albert Museum staged 'Conducting Shakespeare', a bizarre experiment which got chaps with glasses and white coats frightfully excited.

The premise of the event was as follows: the eggheads in charge selected 18 of Shakespeare's most emotive and rousing speeches, including the balcony scene from *Romeo and Juliet*, one of Hamlet's diatribes and Macbeth's 'Is this a dagger which I see before me?' soliloquy, and employed a couple of actors to do their thing on stage at the V&A.

The science bit was that they wired up four willing members of the audience with biosensors to measure their heart rate, brain waves, muscle tension and rate of perspiration. From the data supplied, the boffins recorded their guinea pigs' emotional responses to what was unfolding before them and then, on the hoof, chose the next scene to be performed.

The bizarre performance was the brainchild of Alexis Kirke, a member of Plymouth University's Interdisciplinary Centre for Computer Music Research, who had been watching a few of the Bard's most iconic scenes on *YouTube* and thought a bit of technology could help stitch them all together in a revolutionary new way.

'I was shocked by the emotional intensity of watching these on a computer screen, in a room, on headphones', he explained. 'It just inspired me to make this work. I want to bring a machine into the heart of this intensely human process, into something some people would say is the ultimate artistic expression of humanity. The idea is to conduct these to create a certain emotional arc. It's almost like you can plot emotion on a graph, though of course you can't do that. I feel like I'm almost a performer, playing the actors as instruments.'

'Conducting Shakespeare' was in truth only a partial success however, with the audience jolly impressed by the aforementioned 'emotional arc' which was presented to them, but they were less than enamoured when the performance was suspended for ten minutes when Kirke had to recharge his laptop.

PLASTIC NOT ALWAYS FANTASTIC

2015

Earlier we explored how the lack of a contemporary, verified portrait of the Bard (see 'Picture Imperfect, 1856') means we cannot be sure what Will really looked like. The little beard, the moustache, the big collar and the mullet have become indelibly imprinted on our mind's eye as Shakespeare, but for all we truly know he could have been as bald as a coot, suffered from a lazy left eye and regular outbreaks of acne.

Still, people like the popular image of Will, the 'Chandos' Shakespeare, and should you be so inclined you can even enter Shakespeare lookalike competitions. That's presumably the 'traditional' Bard look they're after rather than your own historical interpretation of his features.

The Southern Shakespeare Company over in Florida hosted a lookalike event in 2015. 'If you look like the Bard, or can transform yourself into him, there are some serious prizes for this not-so-serious competition,' read the blurb on the website. 'Hemingway is easy! The Bard is hard. There will be two categories: "Genuine Will" (that means you actually *look* like him), and "Creative Will" (that means you can do *wonders* with makeup and costumes).'

There was a $500 cash prize for the winner of the 'Genuine Will' category (and a mere $250 for the best 'Creative Will') and it would have been an interesting competition had a Chinese chap by the name of Zhang Yiyi decided to enter.

Zhang is a writer. He's also what you might call a

Shakespeare super fan, and such is his obsession with the Bard, that he has shelled out £151,000 on plastic surgery to look more like Will. It took a total of ten operations over three months on his eyes, lips, nose and face for Zhang to get the Stratfordian look he craved, but when he unveiled his painful transformation, his new appearance rather split opinion on the Internet message boards.

'I think he has an excellent physical likeness to Mr Shakespeare,' wrote one admirer. 'His eyes and nose look very similar and he has done it as a tribute. What greater sacrifice could someone make? I think it was a good idea. Anyway, it is his money and he can spend it on what he likes.'

It's a fair point but not everyone was impressed with the results of the surgery. 'It is ridiculous, what a total waste of money,' wrote one naysayer. 'Why would anyone want to do something like this to their face. Personally, I think it is a bit weird. That is a life changing amount of money and I can't see much difference anyway.'

Type 'Zhang Yiyi' into any reputable search engine and you will be able to judge for yourself whether he's now a spitting image of the Bard. At the risk of spoiling the surprise, however, don't get too excited because he looks nothing like him despite his extensive and expensive procedures. He still plans to enter the Southern Shakespeare Company lookalike competition but has wisely opted for the 'Creative Will' category.

BIBLIOGRAPHY

BOOKS

Shakespeare: The Biography, Peter Ackroyd, Vintage 2006

The Arden Shakespeare Miscellany, Jane Armstrong, Arden, 2011

Shakespeare: The Invention of the Human, Harold Bloom, Fourth Estate, 2008

A Brief Anthology of English Literature, Sammy R. Browne, 2012

Shakespeare the Player, Alexander Cargill, Leopold Classic Library, 2015

The Shakespeare Riots: Revenge, Drama, and Death in Nineteenth-century America, Nigel Cliff, Random House, 2007

The Shakespeare Miscellany, Ben Crystal and David Crystal, Penguin, 2005

Shakespeare, Russell A. Fraser, Transaction Publishers, 2007

Women as Hamlet: Performance and Interpretation in Theatre, Who's Who in Shakespeare: A Dictionary of Characters and Proper Names, Francis Griffin Stokes, Dover Publications, 2011

Film and Fiction, Tony Howard, Cambridge University Press, 2009

Curse of Macbeth and Other Theatrical Superstitions, Richard Huggett, Picton, 1981

Citizen Shakespeare: A Social and Political Portrait, James C. Humes, University Press of America, 2003

Shakespeare's Bones, C.M. Ingleby, Amazon Media, 2012

The Truth Will Out: Unmasking the Real Shakespeare, Brenda James and Professor William Rubinstein, Routledge, 2006

Shakespeare: His Life, Work, and Era, Dennis Kay, Quill, 1994

The Oxford Handbook of Shakespeare, Arthur F. Kinney, OUP Oxford, 2014

Shakespeare and the Countess: The Battle that Gave Birth to The Globe, Chris Laoutaris, Penguin, 2015

The Methuen Drama Dictionary of the Theatre, Jonathan Law, Methuen Drama, 2011

Shakespeare and the Second World War: Memory, Culture, Identity, Irena Makaryk, University of Toronto Press , 2012

Recritiquing William Shakespeare, Amar Nath Prasad, Amazon Media, 2012

Shakespeare's Family, Kate Pogue, Praeger, 2008

William Shakespeare: A Compact Documentary Life, Samuel Schoenbaum, Oxford University Press, 1992

Shakespeare's Imagery and What it Tells Us, Caroline F.E. Spurgeon, Cambridge University Press, 1935

Who Killed William Shakespeare? The Murderer, The Motive, The Means, Simon Andrew Stirling, The History Press, 2013

A Complete Bibliography of Fencing and Duelling, Carl A. Thimm, Naval and Military Press, 1896

The Oxford Companion to Shakespeare, Stanley Wells and Michael Dobson, Oxford University Press, 2009

WEBSITES

www.bbc.co.uk
www.dailymail.co.uk
www.elizabethan-era.org.uk
www.elizabethanenglandlife.com
www.everything-theatre.co.uk
www.findingshakespeare.co.uk
www.historytoday.com
www.imdb.com
www.literarygenius.info
www.pbs.org
www.rememberingshakespeare.com
www.rsc.org.uk
www.shakespeare-online.com
www.shakespeareauthorshipquestion.org
www.shakespearemag.com
www.shakespearesglobe.com
www.shakespeareswords.com
www.strangehistory.net
www.telegraph.co.uk

OTHER TITLES IN

THE STRANGEST SERIES

The *Strangest* series has been delighting and enthralling readers for decades with weird, exotic, spooky and baffling tales of the absurd, ridiculous and the bizarre. This range of fascinating books – from Football to London, Rugby to Law and many subjects in between – details the very curious history of each one's funniest, oddest and most compelling characters, locations and events.

9781910232910

9781910232866

GOLF'S
STRANGEST°
ROUNDS

KENT'S
STRANGEST°
TALES

9781910232934

9781910232972

LAW'S
STRANGEST°
CASES

LONDON'S
STRANGEST°
TALES

9781910232897

9781910232880

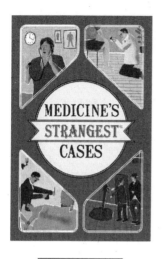

9781910232941

9781910232965

9781910232873

9781910232927

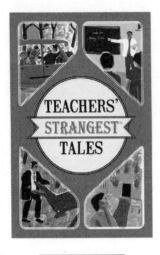

9781910232989

9781910232958

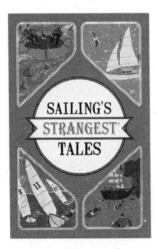

9781911042259